A Global History of the Twentieth Century

A Global History of the Twentieth Century

Legacies and Lessons from Six National Perspectives

Editors
Michael J. Green
Nicholas Szechenyi

Foreword
John J. Hamre

CSIS | CENTER FOR STRATEGIC & INTERNATIONAL STUDIES

ROWMAN & LITTLEFIELD
Lanham • Boulder • New York • London

Center for Strategic & International Studies
1616 Rhode Island Avenue, NW
Washington, DC 20036
202-887-0200 | www.csis.org

Published by Rowman & Littlefield
A wholly owned subsidiary of The Rowman & Littlefield Publishing
Group, Inc.
4501 Forbes Boulevard, Suite 200, Lanham, MD 20706
www.rowman.com

Unit A, Whitacre Mews, 26-34 Stannary Street, London SE11 4AB

ISBN: 978-1-4422-7970-4 (cloth alk. paper)
ISBN: 978-1-4422-7971-1 (paperback)
ISBN: 978-1-4422-7972-8 (electronic)

Contents

FOREWORD

John J. Hamre

The government of Japan (GOJ) first approached the Center for Strategic and International Studies (CSIS) to lead this effort to review the
history of the twentieth century from different national perspectives. I had not previously considered such a question, but it has
resulted in an intellectually rich experience for all of us. In agreeing
to undertake the project, we stipulated two conditions. First, CSIS
would pick all the historians and manage the process independent
of the GOJ. Second, I said the project has to be about the future, not
just the past. The twentieth century was filled by great tragedies. It
also saw the most remarkable boost in standards of living for the
largest number of people in history. What does this tell us about
how to navigate the challenges of the twenty-first century?

I am a political scientist, not an historian. The six historical narratives of the book are rich in important detail. A political scientist,
however, seeks to extract an understanding of the underlying forces
that shape personal and national behavior. Historians will find my
summary deficient, but I hope readers will use this chapter to draw
their own conclusions and find direction for the future.

As several of the historians have noted, the twentieth century
did not begin crisply in 1900. Three major forces shaped the early
decades of the twentieth century, and each of them has origins in
the second half of the nineteenth century.

First, the later decades of the nineteenth century witnessed the
deterioration and eventual collapse of major political structures
that dominated global politics for three centuries. The Habsburg

Empire, the Romanov dynasty, the Qing dynasty, and the Ottoman Empire were in various stages of deterioration, as were the Spanish, British, and French and Dutch metropolitan systems. The remit of power in regions controlled by these empires was in terminal decline.

Second, the global economy was transformed by the wide introduction of steam-powered (and, by 1910, diesel-powered) sea transport and by transoceanic cable communications. Passengers can now book transport on a published schedule, knowing with certainty the dates of departure and arrival. International mail became relatively inexpensive. Newspapers posted journalists around the world, communicating "flash" news via telegraph cable and deeper analysis within days via post. This caused a significant rise in political consciousness around the world. For example, the Japanese defeat of Russia in 1905 gave inspiration to nationalist forces in India and Turkey.

These two fundamental developments gave energy to the third—the rise of nationalist elites who sought to define a future for their country, drawing inspiration from developments in distant lands and using that knowledge to shape a political narrative of national identity and political independence. The colonial playbook to educate the children of elites in the colonies created a cadre of nationalist leaders who sought their own base of power, appropriating national themes to draw popular support.

The first two decades of the twentieth century were politically turbulent. World War I touched off the fundamental transition that was long in waiting. The war broke apart almost all of the empires and started the clock to dismantlement of the rest.

The global depression in the 1930s caused tension and stress everywhere. National governments sought to find ways to insulate themselves from forces that transcended parochial sovereign power. National leaders then lacked the tools to manage local impacts of a global recession, and leaders undertook urgent measures to manage popular discontent. The Great Depression gave rise to fascism, communism, nationalism, and isolationism, each offering competing solutions to these strains. Each of these political philosophies found grounding in various countries, leading ultimately to the tragedy of World War II.

World War II finally broke the hold of empires, creating nearly a hundred new countries struggling to define their respective futures. The two great factions that emerged after World War II, the Atlantic Community, led by the United States and Western Europe, and the Warsaw Pact, led by the Soviet Union, competed for the loyalties of these new countries. The United States championed a liberal international order that tolerated local independent political expression more effectively than did the international communist system. This led to an explosion of economic vitality, innovation, and trade in the West that widened the gap between the two camps in terms of resources and legitimacy. Many countries sought to stand outside the competition of the Cold War, but it was not until China broke from Soviet orthodoxy that it found a pathway for economic transformation that brought hundreds of millions of Chinese out of abject poverty.

The first half of the twentieth century was hugely tragic. The second half was remarkable. The last five decades of the twentieth century saw the most remarkable transformation of the human condition for the better than any time in recorded history. Science and technology significantly boosted wellness around the globe. Innovation in agriculture created enormous improvements in diets. International trade brought poor countries into a global economy, significantly boosting living standards. China's transformation was astounding—with 400 million people entering a global middle class and hunger being virtually eliminated.

To what can we attribute the remarkable transformation in the twentieth century between the dark first half and the relatively golden succeeding years? One political feature stands out. The second half of the twentieth century saw the creation of a network of global institutions designed to coordinate national actions to cope with problems that transcended the sovereign remit of any one country. The League of Nations was hobbled from the outset and had no capacity to deal with the economic stress caused by the global depression in the 1930s. The uncoordinated actions by individual nations amplified the recession by championing inappropriate parochial responses.

What surprised me most in reading the essays of the six historians was the insignificance of structured international institutions—the League of Nations and the United Nations—in their respective recounting of history. Nation-states behaved in classic realpolitik modalities throughout the century, little modulated by the international institutions created to prevent a cataclysm experienced twice in the first half of the century. No doubt, a historian of the United Nations system would draw quite different conclusions. But the six historians barely mention the United Nations in recounting their respective narratives.

Yet it seems clear that the second half of the twentieth century was substantially better because there were more effective international mechanisms within the UN "system" to deal with problems of an international scale. The Bretton Woods organizations were created to deal with international financial problems. This pattern of coordination led to much stronger financial coordination mechanisms in the private sector. Government leaders had more tools and greater knowledge about how to manage global financial stress.

The second half of the twentieth century was hardly free of armed conflict. Indeed, there were 54 wars of varying intensity and duration during the last five decades. The great powers skirmished indirectly through proxies in many of these conflicts, but the transcending fear of nuclear war created caution in key capitals. Again, international institutions provided venues for dealing with geopolitical confrontation. Nations are still guided by classic realpolitik interests, but a network of international institutions created many more ways to find solutions.

We are now 15 years into the twenty-first century. As with the start of the twentieth century, there are again fundamental forces shaping the larger structure of political competition in this era.

We are experiencing the dizzying impact of technology on modern life. Communication technology now permits globe-spanning business models that take advantage of engineering talent in one continent and comparatively inexpensive labor in a distant continent. American workers now compete against workers in distant lands. Cell phones have become ubiquitous, and cameras on cell phones make political developments known almost instantaneously on a global basis. Global transportation systems—created by the advent of container sea transport and intermodal aggregation and disaggregation of shiploads of containers—created globe-spanning supply chains and streamlined national customs procedures. Good things (manufactured goods, capital, tourism) and bad things (terrorism, human trafficking, illegal drugs, pollution) alike move internationally with unprecedented ease.

The ease of movement of goods, capital, and ideas is now causing a new rise of global consciousness. At the start of the twentieth century, the rise of global political consciousness was limited to elites who could travel internationally and had educational levels that gave them access to knowledge in distant lands. At the start of the twenty-first century, political consciousness is rising from the base of political societies. A desperate Tunisian immolates himself and within days popular protests break out around the Arab world. Six terrorists in Paris slaughter innocent citizens and change the consciousness of vulnerability throughout Europe.

Unlike the twentieth century, which began with the collapse of the international political order, the twenty-first century is not experiencing the collapse of historic political systems. With the exception of the Middle East, where the legitimacy of governments is uncertain from the perspective of popular sentiment, most governments around the world enjoy legitimacy with their respective citizenry. But there are global challenges of political significance, even for countries with stable and legitimate government systems.

Two major questions loom before us, however. The first is the ability of nation-states to respond to politically charged actions of nonstate actors. The second is the diminished vitality of the formal structures of international coordination created in the early days after World War II. I will deal with each in turn.

The first great challenge of this era concerns the ability of national governments to manage information that has political significance domestically, and to chart a course of action that seems appropriate and timely. One hundred years ago governments had greater capacity to manage and shape public understanding of problems. Citizens had a bias to look to government leaders to interpret the meaning of events and ideas. News sources were more limited and sought to understand the nature of a problem first by asking governments. Today, governments struggle to respond in a timely manner to developments when private voices are loud and instantaneous. It is interesting to note that authoritarian governments are far better at exploiting social media than are popular polities. The internal dynamics of popular polities by definition require extended deliberation to formulate "official" commentary. In the intervening period, private voices have shaped and reshaped popular understanding of developments.

The second problem concerns the vitality of the international institutions created in the early years after World War II. One of the lessons of the twentieth century was the way individual national actions amplified the impact of the Great Depression through inappropriate national policies and a universal "beggar thy neighbor" approach. All of the genuinely difficult issues today—terrorism, crime, illegal drugs, pollution, climate change, diseases like Ebola, human trafficking—are "horizontal," and government structures are "vertical." The migration crisis in Europe is a good example. People rarely want to leave their homeland, but poverty and war cause people to choose to move. But poverty in a distant land rarely motivates politicians to undertake politically difficult measures.

The Ebola crisis in Africa in 2014–2015 highlighted the relative weakness of the World Health Organization. The migration crisis in Europe has hugely challenged the legitimacy and effectiveness of the European Union. The United Nations has been unable to manage the crisis in Ukraine, and no other international body has legitimacy or capability to step in. Arguably, the resolution of the Iranian nuclear weapons program is a counter-indication of success, but the jury is still out as to the long-term success of the agreement.

These two problems are not unrelated. International problems often become domestic problems with different manifestations. The inability of the government to deal with international problems exacerbates the legitimacy of domestic response and complicates the latency problem. The Ebola crisis likely did contribute in some degree to the Republican takeover of the U.S. Senate in 2014. The rise of the Islamic State is a constant refrain in the ongoing American political debate.

As we survey the twentieth century, the transcending message is the positive role that effective intergovernmental institutions played in providing venues for resolving international problems. These institutions, however, do not effectively deal with the challenges we are facing in the twenty-first century. What is to be done?

There are essentially two modalities of international coordination—structured and irregular. Structural internationalism is grounded on legal instruments and often with standing secretariats to sustain the coordination. Obviously the UN system and the Bretton Woods financial institutions are premier examples of structural internationalism.

The inherent strength of structural internationalism is that it is normative for future generations. The next generation inherits the structure and the momentum of action within the institution. Other organizations—especially nongovernmental organizations—can amplify their power by manipulating the normative powers of structural international institutions. Nothing highlights that better than the climate change agenda that climaxed in Paris with the 21st Conference of the Parties (COP-21) in December 2015.

The problem with structural internationalism is that it takes considerable effort to create the structure, and over time the structure becomes brittle and progressively less legitimate. Again, the United Nations is a good example. The architects of the UN system attempted to reconcile two competing impulses within one institution. The General Assembly embraced broad principals of quality and inclusiveness, organized around the principle of structuring the world we wanted to create. The Security Council—with veto powers given to five countries—was designed to reflect the power geometry that prevailed in 1947. But that structure no longer reflects the power geometry of today. Britain and France are diminished powers, but with veto rights on the Security Council. Germany and Japan, defeated in World War II, now eclipse the power of France and Britain. New powers, such as India and Brazil, have rotating access to the Security Council but no permanent status. The Security Council is reified with no clear path for reform.

The other form of internationalism is irregular—coalitions of the willing. Leaders of countries find colleagues with similar perceptions and agree to work collaboratively to deal with the problem. The advantage of irregular internationalism is the efficiency in creating the coalition and the relative ease of implementing consensus decisions. The deficiency of irregular internationalism is inherent in its advantage. Irregular international organizations are not normative, compared to structural international organizations. A coalition of the willing to deal with one problem rarely becomes the foundation for solving the next problem. The Group of Seven (G7) is a good example. The G7 once was an effective structure for harmonizing activities of the leading industrialized countries. But over time, the G7 has lost its legitimacy, especially for countries near but not in the group. The G20 is arguably more legitimate, but suffers from the same problems for countries 21 and on.

The challenge of the twenty-first century is to find more effective means for coordinating and harmonizing the international response. This will entail strengthening both structural international institutions and reengineering irregular international coalitions. This will take considerable focus and energy, especially for democracies and popular polities. Political leaders rarely find positive electoral benefit focusing on strengthening international organizations. But in the longer term, a nation's ability to cope with transcending problems will directly impact the legitimacy of popular governments. It is worth the energy it will take to create more viable international institutions to augment domestic response in times of crisis.

1. INTRODUCTION

Michael J. Green

In the twentieth century the Eurocentric global order collapsed. The apparent moral authority and legitimacy of empire was replaced by a new political consciousness and competing narratives of injustice and grievance. By century's end, two world wars and a generation of nuclear-imposed restraint had midwifed a more stable international order. Over the course of the century, hundreds of millions were killed by leaders who abused or failed to understand the revolutions in technology and social mobilization, while billions of others were liberated from poverty, racism, and oppression. The trauma of the twentieth century remains deeply imprinted on major powers as they strive to define the rules of the twenty-first century.

This is particularly true of Japan, which transitioned from being one of the most revisionist and violent challengers of the existing international order in East Asia to one of the pillars of postwar peace and prosperity. As the Japanese government prepared to issue a statement on the 70th anniversary of the end of the Pacific War, the Prime Minister's Office established a number of scholarly groups within Japan to reflect on the entirety of the twentieth century in order to understand the larger global currents that shaped Japan's darkest chapter and then to derive lessons for modern times. CSIS was asked to convene a group of historians from around the world who would do parallel research on how different interpretations of global history and national experiences in the twentieth century might contribute to this discourse. As John Hamre explains in the foreword to this volume, we accepted on the condition that we have freedom to select the scholars, to protect their own interpretations of the past, to apply the lessons to contemporary challenges in global governance and statecraft, and to publish this volume independently.

This edited volume features scholars who explore the national experiences of six major powers in the twentieth century to discern the legacies for order today and the lessons for tomorrow. These six powers are the United States, Japan, Turkey, China, India, and Germany:

- The United States, still the lynchpin of international order despite a relative decline in power, entered the twenty-first century with a triumphant national ideology but enormous difficulties defining national purpose in a world returning to a multipolarity reminiscent of the nineteenth century.
- Japan, having embraced the darkest aspects of nineteenth-century empires in defiance of the West, has instead sought power and legitimacy as a champion of Western norms, yet remains shackled by the historical memory of its closest neighbors.
- Turkey, once a member of the imperial club, is burdened by rejection from that club and increasing disorder within its own former imperial space.
- China, which embraced communism and decolonization as the future, rejected both in favor of a performance-based legitimacy that increasingly leaves the Communist Party dependent on nationalist narratives about the past.
- India, in contrast, successfully embraced democracy as the future, but has yet to establish the performance-based legitimacy that would leave postcolonial insecurities in the past.
- Germany, which self-immolated in the Second World War with the most intense nationalism and neo-imperialism of an older era, afterward led in the creation of a postwar order that embraced a vision of peaceful regional integration, only to see that new European order wracked by a new wave of ethnic nationalism from within and without.

How then will these six powers define their roles as power shifts and norms are again contested in the second decade of the twenty-first century? The answer will depend in large part on their interpretations of the twentieth century. Will national leaders retreat to narratives of resentment and grievance or past glory? Or will they assess the forces of change in the twentieth century and apply those lessons to the current era?

The historians and policymakers who produced this volume hope for the second scenario, but recognize how powerful national narratives of history must be for any leader in this era of instantaneous communication and networked emoting.

Many historians would ask why an arbitrary date on the calendar should define an epoch, when other starting points might have been chosen, such as the First World War, or other end points, such as the collapse of the Berlin Wall. The answer, for the purpose of this volume, is that we seek to understand the 70th anniversary of the end of the Second World War in the larger context of what came before. The major antagonists in that conflict did not launch their racial, ideological, and economic conflagration like football players jumping to action when the referee blew the whistle. There was a prehistory that arguably goes back centuries but certainly can be traced from the changing distribution of power and legitimacy a generation before the world wars. Nor were the victors in those wars, particularly the United States, unengaged innocents before 1941. A historical perspective that begins in August 1945 with "in-nations" and "out-nations" ignores the critical lessons of failure in the global system and domestic politics that came before the war and the advances and setbacks that followed.

In order to stitch together the distinctive journeys of each of the states covered in this volume, the authors have each reflected on four dominant global experiences in the twentieth century: (1) economic development and technological progress; (2) global conflicts (World War I, World War II, and the Cold War); (3) global order and institution building; and (4) social revolutions (such as anticolonialism, socialism, nationalism, justice, and women's empowerment).

ECONOMIC DEVELOPMENT AND
TECHNOLOGICAL PROGRESS

The economic and technological tale of the twentieth century is one of accelerated dominance by the West followed at century's end by the shift of economic output—but not yet leadership in technological innovation—to the East. In the nineteenth century, economic output shifted to Western Europe with the Industrial Revolution and the decline of the Qing dynasty and the Ottoman Empire. By the middle of the twentieth century the center of economic output was transatlantic, driven by the rapid rise of American economic power. After 1970, economic output was increasingly distributed around three poles: North America, Europe, and rising East Asia. Yet while globalization has defined geoeconomics in the last three decades of the twentieth century, it also accelerated regionalism in Europe, North America, and East Asia. Only in the twenty-first century did it become evident that regionalism may have reached diminishing returns in Europe, while historic rivalries created in Asia what South Korean president Park Geun-hye called "the Asian paradox" of growing intraregional trade and mutual distrust.

The six states in this study either came to dominance because of these economic trends, were forced to catch up, or were sidelined. The United States became the leading engine of global growth and, in the postwar years, the main steward of globalization. Japan and Germany quickly took advantage of the new postwar open trading order, with China and India to follow. Yet the intersection of globalization and national growth never fully left behind nationalism. Japan's nineteenth-century Meiji example of creating a "rich nation/ strong army" had a profound impact on China. As Chen Jian points out, for China, economic growth in the wake of Deng Xiaoping's opening and reform became the ultimate demonstration of Mao Zedong's claim in 1949 that "we the Chinese have stood up." And, of course, economic growth together with the embrace of democratic norms was Japan's own source of restored legitimacy and influence after 1945. For its part, India's growth was hobbled by postcolonial Nehruvian socialism until China's economic takeoff spurred both the Indian Congress and Bharatiya Janata Party (BJP) governments to focus on growth rather than justice alone as a national economic objective. Turkey began the century with a comparatively wealthy cosmopolitan empire at the intersection of Europe and the Middle East, but fell far behind Europe after the First World War and only began to aspire to European Union membership toward the end of the century—a wish never fulfilled.

GLOBAL CONFLICTS

The twentieth century was characterized by two destructive wars— perhaps not as violent as earlier wars in China or the Thirty Years' War in Europe, but distinctive because of the geographic vastness of the suffering, particularly in the Second World War. As Sebastian Conrad reminds us, the "Cold War" saw equally massive death and suffering, primarily in the form of civil war and social revolution within China. During the Second World War, 65 million people were killed, but the number who died violent deaths over the next half century was close to that number.

The United States was a latecomer to both world wars, but emerged victorious each time: after the first bruised and inward-looking, and after the second determined to prevent Europe or Asia from falling under hostile hegemons ever again. The frame for U.S. participation in the first war—making America safe for democracy—was too lofty to be sustained by the American people so soon after achieving great power status. As William Inboden points out, Franklin Delano Roosevelt's vision for postwar order, expressed in the August 1941 *Atlantic Charter*, reflected Woodrow Wilson's original liberal idealism, but was backed by the great power realism forced on the United States at Pearl Harbor—and ultimately was sustained by Harry Truman's commitment to base U.S. forces at the front lines of freedom in Europe and Asia.

The new Republic of China joined the entente powers in the First World War, hoping to redress historic injustices as a full member of the international community, but the war dashed those hopes by opening a path for the other Asian entente power—Japan—to spread its imperial space after the West weakened itself in Europe. The next world war (begun for Asians with the 1937 Japanese invasion of China) ended with both the Japanese and the Chinese nationalists spent, unleashing the revolutionary Chinese Communist Party on the rest of continental Asia.

Turkey drew the wrong card in both world wars—losing an empire in the first and becoming marginalized in the second. But the Cold War established a new grounding for Turkey's geopolitical status and a legitimacy for Turkish nationalism when juxtaposed against the communist empire to the north. As Cemil Aydin points out, that geopolitical status may ironically have arrested some of the positive social change that had begun decades earlier.

India, meanwhile, was forged as a modern nation-state by the two world wars. In the First World War, Indians developed an unprecedented national consciousness as millions fought side-by-side with regular British regiments in every theater of conflict. Yet hopes for independence after the war were dashed. The Second World War finally gave birth to Indian independence, as British imperialism exhausted itself and the United States and Japan in very different ways demonstrated the inevitability of decolonization. Despite emerging as a victor in every sense from the wars, India was almost as traumatized as the defeated powers—forced to consolidate postcolonial sovereignty and deal with the aftermath of bloody partition. Only with the end of the Cold War did India begin the process of reform and more confident participation in international affairs.

For Germany's political/strategic culture, the two world wars were most transformational. Sebastian Conrad cautions, however, that German scholars have constructed a national narrative of *Sonderweg* (deviance) that obscures the degree to which Germany shaped and was shaped by the events before, during, and after the wars. Even embedding in a common European destiny after the Second World War was not the result of a uniquely German strategy of repentance. It reflected external decisions and factors, including the integration of Western Europe, security concerns in the Cold War, and the narratives for unification afterward. The lesson, in short, is that Germany's remarkable transformation after the war was part of a global history that Germany must shape to be successful in the twenty-first century.

Japan's own version of *Sonderweg* never became a consensus view domestically—and was never abandoned by China (and to some extent Korea) in the 70 years after the war. Japan was propelled by imperialism in the nineteenth century to modernize in order to avoid China's fate. Rather than challenge the West, Japan chose the ultimate source of external legitimization—alliance with Britain and subsequently entry into the First World War on the victor's side. As Shinichi Kitaoka and Yuichi Hosoya point out, the 1920s were an era of relative stability, liberalism, and convergence for Japan, based on the assumption that economic progress would forever prevent a repetition of global war. However, when the global economic order collapsed and Bolshevism rose to confront the vestiges of imperialism and capitalism, resentful Japanese leaders rejected economic conversion and embraced totalitarianism—much like Germany and Turkey. Emerging in a postwar Asia as part of the democratic camp confronting totalitarianism on the continent of Asia, the anti-Bolshevik dimension of Japan's wartime aggression retained elements of legitimacy within the new conservative leadership. Thus Japan's postwar pacifism was as much a result of international power politics and the goal of restoring autonomy through economic growth as it was a process of internally driven cleansing. Japan in the twenty-first century must again help shape or be shaped by international events.

GLOBAL ORDER AND INSTITUTIONS

The twentieth century began with the final disintegration of the Concert of Europe under which imperial dynasties had maintained peace for the purpose of mutual survival. In the interwar years, institution building designed to restore a new order based on laws rather than aristocratic understandings briefly succeeded. But these rickety institutions such as the League of Nations and the Washington Naval Conference could not survive under tentative American leadership alone, as European power waned and new nationalist consciousness arose in Europe's empires and Asia. It was a great triumph of human development that postwar order rested in part on the establishment of institutions in which the leading powers agreed to cede some degree of their economic and political autonomy to sustain the system.

The United States may have proven the most instrumental and damaging of these six states with respect to efforts at institutionalizing order in the twentieth century. As William Inboden notes, American exceptionalism led to bold attempts to create institutions such as the League of Nations, but then contributed to their demise as the U.S. Congress rejected entanglement with the rest of the world. The lesson of America's failed global institution building made a profound imprint on the architects of postwar strategy and the United Nations and Bretton Woods systems. Yet Truman and those "present at the creation" nevertheless had to overcome considerable resistance from Congress to these expanded international obligations, a challenge that has faced every president as U.S. economic power has shrunk from 50 percent of global output to a fifth. Indeed, the U.S.-led postwar neoliberal order was only possible because of the commitment of the former enemies, such as Japan and Germany, to the new liberal international system.

China has benefited enormously from the open institutional order established after the Second World War, yet has never fully embraced its legitimacy. From the perspective of the modern Chinese Communist Party, the stage should have been set by the spheres of influence and destruction of Japanese power seemingly established by the Yalta and Potsdam Conferences (so much so that modern Chinese propaganda teaches students that Mao rather than Chiang Kai-shek attended the earlier summit at Cairo). Yet the 1951 San Francisco Treaty negotiations—to which Communist China was not invited—put Japan at the center of an alliance system aimed at containing Chinese and Soviet power. The Sino-Soviet split, Sino-U.S. rapprochement, and China's opening to Western economic development all changed that; power politics vis-à-vis the Soviets led Japan and China to shelve historic grievances in pursuit of mutual economic gain and realpolitik. Still, Beijing never fully accepted the legitimacy of the San Francisco System, which remains central to U.S. strategy to this day and a burr in Sino-U.S. relations and Sino-Japanese relations.

India was the only non-self-governing state to sign the Treaty of Versailles and join the League of Nations after the First World War; it then joined the United Nations, the World Bank, and the International Monetary Fund during and after the Second World War. Yet India's fierce resistance to interference in internal affairs often put Delhi in the position of opposing Western efforts to establish a more open and rules-based international order.

The story of institution building in the twentieth century is thus one of remarkable success in the postwar years, but also stunning lapses in leadership by the leading powers and rejection by rising powers. These lessons must not be lost as the Bretton Woods system comes under increasing stress from shifting power balances in the twenty-first century.

SOCIAL REVOLUTIONS

No state was left untouched by social revolution in the twentieth century. Technological change empowered women, minorities, and colonized states. Global war reordered power at home just as it did abroad, weakening the legitimacy of class, gender, and racial hierarchy.

The United States, born of revolution, was actually least revolutionized by the experiences of the twentieth century. Yet participation in the world wars brought women and minorities into the workforce and political participation, while the Vietnam War spawned generational rebellion. All of this would be propelled by expanding powers for the federal government that would spawn counteractions from the right in the 1980s and even more so today.

National identities also rose from the social revolutions spawned by war and technological change in the twentieth century. Narratives of grievance and injustice drove nationalism and eventually revisionism against the prevailing Anglo-American order in China, Germany, Japan, India, and Turkey at various points. Japan and

Germany embraced the British example of imperialism in the nineteenth century only to be rejected by the original members of the club. For those with no interest in joining the imperial club, Wilsonian idealism appeared at first to offer a separate route to national sovereignty, anticolonialism, and social justice. But by 1921, Wilson's own racist views and the isolationism of the U.S. Congress turned many leaders in the colonialized world toward more radical solutions such as Bolshevism. After the war, Americans struggled to protect democratic norms while simultaneously defending vulnerable states against communist revolution, often by reimposing trappings of old imperialist order. In Vietnam the United States got it wrong, but in Korea, Taiwan, and the Philippines they succeeded.

For nation-states born of grievance and resentment, like China, the narrative of victimhood became essential even after economic growth added a new source of legitimacy. The bloody crackdown in Tiananmen Square in 1989 reflected less the revolutionary instincts of the protesting students than the fear of revolution by party leaders. Parties born of grievance recognized its latent potential. These trends would be driven by the Internet and social media, but these technological factors were only accelerators, barely present in most societies at the end of the twentieth century. Turkey too experienced its century of shame, but restored national identity around a smaller secular republic in 1923. Rather than ending internal struggles for social justice, however, the replacement of a relatively cosmopolitan multiethnic empire with a more ethnically based identity led to decades of struggle by groups now oppressed by Turkish nationalism.

India underwent remarkable demographic change in the twentieth century, more than tripling in population and developing a growing national identity from the experiences of the world wars. And as Srinath Raghavan explains, Gandhi and the Congress Party ensured that this nationalism spread from a small group of British-educated elites in the first decades of the century to the broader masses, thus undermining the Raj's argument that independence would reopen ancient ethnic and religious conflict. This thesis could only work under democracy, and India thus became the first nation-state to bet its existence on democratic governance without first developing an economy. Once again, questions of social justice and order at home became intertwined with the survival of the state internationally. And despite the introduction of universal suffrage in the 1950 constitution, the Indian state continues its struggle to fully empower women, lower castes, and Muslims.

TOWARD A NEW UNDERSTANDING
OF THE TWENTIETH CENTURY

The distinguished scholars in this volume each offer their own interpretation of the twentieth century, both as global historians and as interpreters of their own national experiences. This opening essay has drawn together the cross-cutting themes that are presented in the compelling chapters that follow. The other purpose is to inform readers of the specific lessons for how political leaders and citizens of the world should think about the challenges that confront us all in the twenty-first century.

The bottom-line lesson is that no nation-state is immune from global history or absolved of responsibility for understanding its impact as each state defines its role in a new century. Yet it would be irresponsibly naïve to pretend that leaders will define their purpose based primarily on the global challenges going forward. The tragedies of the twentieth century resulted as states sought to restore sovereignty in the face of global forces beyond their control. This was true of democracies and totalitarian states alike, though each took separate paths (particularly before the Second World War when the democracies turned inward and the totalitarian states searched for enemies at home and abroad). Looking at world leaders across the globe today, there is little room for optimism that this next century will automatically be different. The key to statecraft will therefore be in defining a common global agenda that leaders believe will make their own states fundamentally stronger.

2. LIFTING THE BURDENS OF THE PAST: HOW THREE MID-TWENTIETH-CENTURY PRESIDENTS TRANSFORMED THE UNITED STATES

William Inboden

For a still relatively young nation, the United States bears heavily the burdens of history. America's self-identity and global posture in the early decades of the twenty-first century are shaped indelibly by the nation's past. So also its continuing internal debates over America's international policies and role are often arguments about history.

While the seventeenth-century Puritan settlements, eighteenth-century American founding, and nineteenth-century Civil War all continue to exert tremendous influence on the national consciousness, it is the twentieth century that played a determinative role in forging the United States as it is today. During the twentieth century, Americans wrestled with a series of conflicts that often posed their nation's extant traditions against profound new challenges. External changes in the international system and internal changes in American society each clashed with the nation's received practices. While eventually the United States navigated these challenges successfully and in the process created new national narratives and new traditions, the transitions were often agonizing, costly, and wracked with conflict. That America was able to adapt and emerge stronger bears testimony to many factors, but three stand out:

political leadership, an honest reckoning by citizens, and the iden-
tification of historical resources that helped steer the transition.

Conceptually the United States underwent two transitions in the
twentieth century as it confronted and then departed from two of
its peculiar historical traditions. In the international realm, the
United States transitioned from isolationism to internationalism,
and in the domestic realm from exclusive intolerance to inclusive
pluralism. In turn each of these conceptual transitions had specific
policy and cultural manifestations. Internationally, the United
States moved from eschewing international commitments to embracing, even creating, multilateral institutions and formal treaty
alliances, and from a global posture of withdrawal to engagement
and international leadership. Domestically, the United States transitioned from a hierarchical exclusivity that privileged white Protestants while marginalizing and discriminating against other races
and religions, to an inclusive and pluralistic society that extended
civil rights to all regardless of race, ethnicity, or creed.

While these transitions took place over the course of the century,
they are most intensely focused during the middle three decades
of the century: the period from 1932 to 1960. And while many
American political, religious, intellectual, and civic leaders played
important roles, three U.S. presidents stand out as indispensable:
Franklin Delano Roosevelt, Harry S. Truman, and Dwight D. Eisenhower. This chapter will explore the nature of these transitions as
the United States wrestled with its history, assess how these historical
burdens still influence the United States today, and suggest some
potential lessons and insights that might be relevant for other
nations grappling with their own historical legacies.

THREE SACRED TEXTS FROM EARLY AMERICAN HISTORY

For the century and a half from the first English settlements in
North America through to the Revolutionary era, the formation of
the American identity included the development of traditions and
values that carried within themselves internal tensions and the seeds
of later divisions. In many ways the debates of the mid-twentieth

century were at their core arguments over history: What did America's past mean, and how should it guide the United States on matters of international politics, war and peace, and citizenship?

One seminal tradition in American history dates to Puritan leader John Winthrop's "City on a Hill" sermon. In 1630 while sailing to the New World aboard the ship *Arbella*, Winthrop invoked the Gospel of Matthew in proclaiming to his fellow Puritans: "We shall find that the God of Israel is among us . . . when He shall make us a praise and glory that men shall say of succeeding plantations, 'may the Lord make it like that of New England.' For we must consider that we shall be as a city upon a hill. The eyes of all people are upon us."[1] In his call for their new community to be a "city upon a hill," Winthrop provided one of the most enduring and powerful themes in American history—that of the United States as the exceptional nation. Countless political leaders, famously including John F. Kennedy and Ronald Reagan, have appropriated Winthrop's phrase in urging a special role for America in the world.

But the frequent invocation of the "city on a hill" image glosses over its contested meaning. Specifically, should the United States just be a model to the rest of the world, or does the United States have a mission to the rest of the world? American leaders who favor a more restrained role in the world, if not outright isolationism, have taken the former interpretation, whereas those who believe in a more active role of international engagement and leadership embrace the "city on a hill" imagery to mandate an American mission to the world.

A second American founding document with a contested meaning has been the Declaration of Independence. With its revolutionary assertion, "We hold these truths to be self-evident, that all men are created equal, that they are endowed by their Creator with certain unalienable Rights, that among these are Life, Liberty, and the pursuit of Happiness," the Declaration's emphatic eloquence belied the fierce debates over its meaning.[2] Two contests were especially pronounced and consequential and came to define many subsequent conflicts in the nation, including a civil war. First, did the Declaration's proclamation of human equality apply to all human beings or only to white male property holders, given the political realities of the day in a slaveholding nation? This question became especially acute with the ratification of the Constitution in the next decade, with its perverse classification of slaves as only "three-fifths" of a person. Second, did it apply only to American citizens, or to all persons around the world?

The third canonical document from the founding era is President George Washington's Farewell Address. The full text and thrust of Washington's 1796 message to the American people is more subtle and complex than its historical caricature, but its most famous passage—"It is our true policy to steer clear of permanent alliances with any portion of the foreign world"—accurately summarizes one of Washington's paramount concerns.[3] This in turn defined a tradition in American foreign policy that endured for at least a century, and longer in some incarnations. In the words of historian Walter MacDougall,

> unless the United States remained at Liberty to pick and choose its foreign involvements, it would become entwined in the alliances and alignments of the European powers, see its interests trampled by enemies or betrayed by allies, risk reopening the American continents to the play of competing empires, and bow to the necessity of maintaining an army and navy far in excess of Washington's "suitable establishment on a respectable defensive posture"—all of which would tend to compromise Americans' first and dearest tradition, their independence and commitment to Liberty, however they might choose to define it.[4]

These three documents encapsulated three debates that consumed the United States for the first 150 years of its existence as a nation. As a "city on a hill," was America a mere model removed from the world or did it have an active mission to the world? Did the Declaration of Independence promise equality just to a certain class of American citizens or to all human beings? Did Washington's farewell address mean the United States should avoid international institutions and alliances forever, or just during the precarious early years of its existence as a small nation threatened by European great power politics?

The ensuing century and a half would bring heated conflicts over these questions, including a Civil War that tore the nation asunder, but the disputes themselves would not be resolved until the middle of the twentieth century. Then the threat of totalitarianism forced the United States to confront, and answer, these unresolved burdens of its past. While these debates played out in the halls of Congress, in the editorial pages of newspapers, and in houses of worship, community centers, and homes across the nation, ultimately their resolution depended on the political leadership residing in the White House. And while these may appear to be a discrete set of questions and debates, in practice the conflicts of the twentieth century forced all of these disputes together into a tumultuous cauldron, where the resolutions of each interacted with and shaped the outcomes of others.

FRANKLIN DELANO ROOSEVELT AND THE MOVE FROM ISOLATIONISM TO INTERNATIONALISM

While scholars such as Robert Kagan and Max Boot have demonstrated that the United States did not spend the nineteenth century in pure isolation from the rest of the world, it remains true that, by and large during that era, the young nation focused its attentions and energies on consolidating its control of the continent and studiously avoiding entanglement in European great power contests or traditional colonial adventures abroad.[5] This changed somewhat in the first two decades of the twentieth century, particularly as Presidents Theodore Roosevelt and Woodrow Wilson dramatically expanded the international role of the United States. (Despite their mutual contempt for each other, they actually shared a commitment to America's international engagement, albeit through different means and for different ends.) Thus Teddy Roosevelt followed his predecessor William McKinley's acquisition of colonial territories in the 1898 Spanish-American War by consolidating American control of the Philippines, Cuba, and Hawaii. Roosevelt also projected American influence and power abroad through his mediation of the

Portsmouth Treaty ending the Russo-Japanese War, his diplomacy and construction of the Panama Canal, or by sailing the Great White Fleet of U.S. battleships on a then-unprecedented round-the-world voyage. Wilson, meanwhile, led the United States into World War I not to restore a continental balance of power but to "make the world safe for democracy." His idealistic vision of collective security, free trade, self-determination, and international law, embodied in the League of Nations, in turn was predicated on sustained international leadership by the United States. As visionary as this was in its own right, it was even more audacious given that it depended on the United States jettisoning its previous posture of detachment from international politics.

And it was not to be. The United States Senate, channeling a significant sector of popular sentiment, famously rejected the Treaty of Versailles and American membership in the League of Nations. The carnage of World War I and the dashed hopes of Versailles combined to prompt many Americans to return to what they believed was their nation's natural, principled, and most advantageous posture: continental isolation and remove from the ostensibly intractable conflicts of Europe and Asia.

Such was the situation in the 1930s. Notwithstanding Imperial Japan's growing aggression in Asia and Nazi Germany's increasingly assertive territorial demands in Europe, most Americans wanted their nation to abjure involvement in international affairs in general and Asian and European conflicts in particular. Reinforcing this policy of isolationism was the fact that the United States had no formal alliances; no mutual defense treaties existed that would obligate America to fight on behalf of the likes of Great Britain, France, China, or any other nation should it be a victim of aggression. It would seem that the "city on a hill" was just a model to the world, and that Washington's caution against "permanent alliances" was just as binding in 1938 as it was in 1796.

On the domestic front—in a situation that may seem to be separate from international issues but was in fact deeply intertwined—the United States maintained formal and informal institutions of racial and religious prejudice. "Jim Crow" laws in the South segregated black Americans from white Americans in schools, restaurants, housing, public transportation, and virtually every other aspect of everyday life. American Catholics and especially Jews suffered regular discrimination by the predominantly Protestant culture, especially in the elite echelons of a society still dominated by the "WASP" (White Anglo-Saxon Protestant) establishment. This snapshot of American society appeared to reify a reading of the Declaration of Independence's equality passages as only applying to white Protestants.

Yet in these same years that such sentiments seemed to reign supreme, America was governed by a president who sought to lead the nation in a different direction. One of the most artful statesmen ever to occupy the Oval Office, Franklin Delano Roosevelt envisioned an America that was more pluralistic and tolerant at home while showing international leadership and engagement abroad. To be sure, the crafty and elusive president's own beliefs and tactics evolved over the course of the decade. And he faced considerable opposition, from both public opinion and senior political leaders. Into the early years of the 1940s, it took a combination of Roosevelt's deft leadership and the crisis of global war for the nation to embrace a new set of commitments—and in the process to reinterpret its own history.

Public opinion stood in massive opposition to Roosevelt's desire for the United States to support the Allied cause. A February 1940 poll found that 77 percent of Americans opposed entry into World War II to help rescue Britain and France from defeat—a figure especially notable given that Nazi Germany had already invaded Poland and threatened the rest of Europe.[6] Nor did the American people even support humanitarian gestures that did not involve military deployments or international commitments. A vivid example of how foreign policy isolationism merged with racial and religious intolerance came in a 1939 poll where 61 percent of Americans opposed the Wagner-Rogers Bill that would have provided asylum to 20,000 German Jewish children attempting to flee Nazi persecution.[7] Heeding, and often sharing, public opinion, Congress rejected the bill.

Many senior political leaders of both political parties reinforced America's isolation. In the January 1941 debate over Roosevelt's Lend-Lease Act to provide munitions to nations threatened by Nazi aggression (especially Great Britain), Democratic Senator Burton Wheeler warned that "if the American people want a dictatorship— if they want a totalitarian form of government and war, this bill should be steamrolled through Congress, as is the wont of President Roosevelt."[8] Leading Republican Senator Robert Taft made a strategic case for isolationism. "I believe that the peace and happiness of the people of this country," he averred, "can best be secured by refusing to intervene in war outside the Americas and establishing our defense line based on the Atlantic and Pacific Oceans."[9] Taft's sentiments are a good reminder that isolationism was not merely a product of benighted nativism, but had a sophisticated intellectual and historical pedigree.

Yet Roosevelt believed that what may have been an astute policy for the United States in the nineteenth century was in fact a strategically perilous course to follow in 1940. The United States was now too powerful, and the world too dangerous, for America to stay secluded in its hemispheric repose. To move his nation into the international arena, Roosevelt wielded the tools of rhetoric, legislation, and statecraft. From the late 1930s to 1941, he gave a series of speeches and interviews to prepare the nation and mobilize public opinion for the need to support the allies and what he believed to be America's inevitable entry into the war. In his January 1939 State of the Union address, as part of his call for a substantial increase in military spending, Roosevelt warned, "Storms from abroad directly challenge three institutions indispensable to Americans, now as always. The first is religion. It is the source of the other two—democracy and international good faith. . . . There comes a time in the affairs of men when they must prepare to defend, not their homes alone, but the tenets of faith and humanity on which their churches, their governments, and their very civilization are founded."[10] Here Roosevelt deftly integrated multiple concerns. By speaking of the generic "religion" rather than a more specific and sectarian Protestantism, he sought to appeal to Americans of all faiths and implicitly unite them together against the threat of totalitarianism. He also connected turmoil and aggression abroad with threats to American values and security at home, implicitly building the rationale for the United States to support countries threatened by Germany and Japan.

Roosevelt would also appeal to American history. Not content to leave the country's historical narrative to his isolationist opponents, Roosevelt frequently employed different interpretations of history that highlighted the need for American leadership and resistance to tyranny. Thus his September 21, 1939, message to Congress pointed out that America's historic neutrality had always permitted trade with belligerent nations—with one calamitous exception:

> Beginning with the foundation of our constitutional Government in the year 1789, the American policy in respect to belligerent nations, with one notable exception, has been based on international law. Be it remembered that what we call international law has always had as its primary objectives the avoidance of causes of war and the prevention of the extension of war. The single exception to which I refer was the policy adopted by this nation during the Napoleonic Wars, when, seeking to avoid involvement, we acted for some years under the so-called Embargo and Non-Intercourse Acts. That policy turned out to be a disastrous failure—first, because it brought our own nation close to ruin, and, secondly, because it was the major cause of bringing us into active participation in European wars in our own War of 1812. It is merely reciting history to recall to you that one of the results of the policy of embargo and non-intercourse was the burning in 1814 of part of this Capitol in which we are assembled today. Our next deviation by statute from the sound principles of neutrality, and peace through international law did not come for one hundred and thirty years. It was the so-called Neutrality Act of 1935.[11]

Here Roosevelt contended that just as America's refusal to trade with European nations during the Napoleonic Wars had harmed the

United States, so now Congress's Neutrality Act preventing U.S. sales of munitions to Great Britain threatened similar malefactions. And he wrong-footed the isolationists by pointing out that America's historic "neutrality" did not mean withdrawal from international commerce.

Even as Roosevelt increased America's support for Great Britain while also bolstering military spending to prepare his nation for war, he simultaneously began laying the foundation for the postwar. He envisioned a new international political and economic order of multilateral institutions, with the United Nations as a centerpiece and the United States in the dominant leadership role. In doing so he drew on some of Wilson's collective security idealism yet sought to avoid the sorry fate of the League of Nations by also accounting for the realities of great power politics. The seeds of this postwar order can be found most explicitly in the Atlantic Charter, a merely 376-word manifesto issued jointly by Roosevelt and British Prime Minister Winston Churchill at the conclusion of their epochal first meeting aboard the cruiser USS *Augusta* in Placentia Bay, Newfoundland. As historian Elizabeth Borgwardt points out, the Atlantic Charter "prefigured the rule-of-law orientation of the Nuremberg Charter, the collective security articulated in the United Nations Charter, and even the free-trade ideology of the Bretton Woods charters that established the World Bank and the International Monetary Fund."[12] As I have written elsewhere, "to this list of Atlantic Charter-inspired ideals and institutions could be added the Marshall Plan, NATO, the G-8, the World Trade Organization, and even the European Union."[13] How could such a short statement of idealistic principles such as "the right of all peoples to choose the form of Government under which they will live," "bring[ing] about the fullest collaboration between all nations in the economic field," and establishing a postwar peace that "should enable all men to traverse the high seas and oceans without hindrance" be so consequential?[14] Because the significance of the Atlantic Charter lies not just in what it said, but especially in *who said it*. In issuing this statement, Roosevelt implicitly committed the United States to upholding it and to leading the construction of a postwar international order that would institutionalize its principles of collective security, an open maritime order, free trade, and respect for human rights and political self-governance. In other words, it pledged the United States to playing an active role in global leadership, international alliances, and upholding universal human equality.

In his customarily subtle and indirect way, Roosevelt also tried to nudge his nation toward a more inclusive realization of religious pluralism and racial equality. While in historical hindsight he was regrettably cautious and slow on racial matters, he did push through some important measures such as the desegregation of defense contractors. Much of the impetus for progress came from the activism of black Americans themselves astutely taking advantage of the tumult of the wartime crisis to press their demands to serve their country. As historian David Kaiser concludes, "Negroes and the labor movement demanded and received some new concessions in return for their participation in the defense of the United States, and they earned capital that paid enormous dividends in the twenty years following the war."[15] Ethnic minorities also earned the grudging respect of their white countrymen through their military service in the shamefully segregated armed services. Most famously, the all-black Tuskegee Airmen of the 332nd Fighter Group and the Japanese-American 442nd Regiment of the U.S. Army both served in combat with distinction and valor and, in the process, dispelled pernicious racial stereotypes.

Religious pluralism enjoyed somewhat greater progress in the war. The "melting pot" of the American military immersed many faiths together and helped erode religious prejudices. The military chaplaincy institutionalized the battlefield equality of Protestants, Catholics, and Jews. Poignant displays of interfaith cooperation and solidarity were exemplified by the "Four Chaplains"—two Protestants, a Catholic, and a Jewish chaplain who all voluntarily gave up their life preservers and thus their lives as they prayed together onboard their sinking ship, the USS *Dorchester*, after it was torpedoed by a German U-Boat in February 1943. The U.S. government devoted significant media and publicity efforts to publicizing the inspiring sacrifice of the chaplains as a vivid display of interfaith unity against the totalitarian foe. This in turn helped cultivate greater attitudes of religious tolerance among the American people, particularly as many American Protestants began to look more favorably on Catholics and Jews.[16]

While much can and should be made of Roosevelt's personal efforts to align his nation behind international engagement abroad and greater protections for human dignity at home, geopolitics also played an essential role in America's unfolding transformation. From 1939 to 1941, the Nazi threat appeared more and more menacing to the United States, especially as Hitler conquered almost all of the European continent and *Wehrmacht* forces advanced deep into the heart of the Soviet Union, coming within miles of Moscow. It was of course Imperial Japan's December 7, 1941, surprise attack on Pearl Harbor that finally solidified America's entry into the Pacific War, and Hitler's declaration of war against America on December 11 ensured the United States would be fighting in the European theater as well.

HARRY S. TRUMAN AND THE INSTITUTIONALIZATION OF ROOSEVELT'S VISION

Fortunately for Roosevelt, his two successors as president shared these same commitments. Part of Roosevelt's rationale for replacing Henry Wallace with Harry Truman as his vice president in 1944 was that Truman better shared Roosevelt's vision of strong American international leadership, unlike the ethereal Wallace, who was suspicious of the exercise of American power. (In 1946 Truman would have to fire Wallace as secretary of commerce after Wallace gave a speech critical of American policy and sympathetic to the Soviet Union.) At the conclusion of World War II, Truman faced the challenge of constructing a viable postwar order that would institutionalize American leadership and engagement abroad, while ensuring that other nations also embraced these multilateral commitments.

The story of Truman's leadership in establishing postwar institutions and initiatives such as the United Nations, the World Bank and other Bretton Woods financial agreements, the Marshall Plan, the peace and security treaty with Japan, and the North Atlantic

Treaty Organization (NATO) is well known. Less remembered is the considerable domestic opposition that Truman faced, from an American public weary of war and still wary of international commitments, and from many influential voices in Congress.

To be sure, at the end of the war Truman had an American public more favorably inclined toward international leadership than five years earlier. An October 1945 survey revealed that 71 percent of Americans wanted their nation to take an active role in world affairs, a number that stayed relatively constant over the next decade.[17] Yet precisely what that role would entail provoked considerable division and disagreement. As the legislative expression of popular sentiment, Congress subjected every major Truman initiative to considerable scrutiny. Despite the urgency of the European needs it was designed to address, the Marshall Plan endured three months of congressional debate before finally being passed. NATO faced even more scrutiny, as the Senate Foreign Relations Committee and its Democratic chairman, Tom Connally, and Republican ranking member, Arthur Vandenberg, expressed considerable skepticism about the treaty's core provision in Article 5 binding the United States to permanent military obligations in Europe—something that the nation had never before assumed in its history.[18] Leading Republican Senator Robert Taft fiercely opposed NATO as a deviation from the traditions of American history, specifically the Monroe Doctrine, which he saw as a preferable model due to its flexibility. In a speech on the Senate floor announcing his opposition to NATO, Taft declared:

> I would favor a Monroe Doctrine for western Europe. But the Atlantic Pact goes much further. It obligates us to go to war if at any time during the next 20 years anyone makes an armed attack on any of the 12 nations. Under the Monroe Doctrine we could change our policy at any time. We could judge whether perhaps one of the countries had given cause for the attack. Only Congress could declare a war in pursuance of the doctrine. Under the new pact the President can take us into war without Congress.[19]

Against such opposition to its initiatives the Truman administration mounted a robust, and ultimately successful, multifront campaign. It deployed some of its leading voices such as Secretary of State George Marshall and his successor Dean Acheson to Capitol Hill for public testimonies and private meetings with recalcitrant senators. It enlisted the editorial pages and columnists of the nation's leading newspapers to make the case for formal alliances and international engagement. And President Truman himself commanded his presidential bully pulpit to great effect. In speeches across the country, Truman's appeals to the American people invoked both history and the divine in a frequent refrain:

> We are faced now with what God Almighty intended us to be faced with in 1920. We are faced with the leadership of the free peoples of the world. We must assume that leadership, if we expect our children not to have to go through the same situation that we had to go through during the last five or six years. Get these things in your mind, and use your influence to do what God Almighty intended us to do: to get the right sort of peace in the world.[20]

Truman's deft use of history connected America's international withdrawal after World War I with the subsequent onset of World War II and warned Americans that a similar return to isolationism could have even more dire consequences, both here and in the hereafter.

Such impassioned appeals by the president, along with creative policy initiatives and cooperation with Congress led by his capable team including George Kennan, James Forrestal, Jack McCloy, Robert Lovett, Paul Nitze, and the aforementioned Marshall and Acheson, eventually carried the day in winning support for the Truman administration's ambitious new international posture for the United States. And geopolitics played an essential role for Truman, as it did with Roosevelt. As the American people and Congress heard these appeals, they also witnessed a disturbing series of events, with the Soviet Union consolidating control over Eastern Europe by installing proxy communist regimes, attempting to choke off access to West Berlin, and detonating its own atomic bomb in 1949. Events in Asia were just as disconcerting: China fell to Mao's communist forces in 1949, and the next year North Korea (aided and encouraged by Stalin and Mao) invaded South Korea. Against the backdrop of so many international crises, the public shifted its attitudes and generally supported the president's appeals for American global leadership, a strengthened military, treaty alliances, and the permanent stationing of American forces overseas. In the words of political scientist Joseph Nye, "If Wilson and Roosevelt broke from American tradition by sending large American armies overseas, Truman was pivotal by keeping them there. He moved foreign policy from 'no entangling alliances' to a permanent presence abroad and a NATO alliance that lasted into the next century."[21]

The Truman administration also took further steps at home to support religious and racial pluralism and inclusivism. Truman became acutely aware of how his own nation's imperfections and racial and religious discrimination hindered its image and credibility abroad. As described by historian Mary Dudziak,

> when nonwhite foreign dignitaries visited the United States and encountered discrimination, it led to serious diplomatic consequences. And as tension between the United States and the Soviet Union increased in the years after the war, the Soviets made effective use of U.S. failings in this area in anti-American propaganda. Concern about the effect of U.S. race discrimination on Cold War foreign relations led the Truman administration to adopt a pro–civil rights posture as part of its international agenda to promote democracy and contain communism.[22]

Truman made this pitch explicit in a landmark 1948 address to Congress on civil rights, admonishing Congress that "if we wish to inspire the peoples of the world whose freedoms are in jeopardy, if we wish to restore hope to those who have already lost their civil liberties, if we wish to fulfill the promise that is ours, we must correct the remaining imperfections in our practice of democracy."[23] While his legislative efforts to pass civil rights measures were stymied by the opposition of segregationist Democrats, Truman did make effective use of executive orders, such as to maintain an anti-discrimination employment commission and, most famously, his 1948 order to desegregate the armed forces.

Truman also sought to promote religious pluralism and tolerance. This Baptist president's opposition to anti-Semitism helped influence his decision to extend diplomatic recognition to the state of Israel at the moment of its creation in 1948, just as his sympathies for Catholicism led him to maintain a diplomatic envoy to the Vatican, over the fierce objections of many American Protestant leaders. For Truman, such initiatives also had a Cold War rationale. His efforts to marshal domestic and international opinion against communism included persistent outreach efforts to American Catholics and Jews, to the point that he spent years of time and political capital trying to forge a pan-religious coalition of Protestants, Catholics, and Jews united against communism.[24] For Truman, moving the United States from isolationism to internationalism and from intolerance to pluralism was essential to America's new grand strategy.

DWIGHT D. EISENHOWER AND
THE BIPARTISAN CONSENSUS

While public support is essential for developing and maintaining new initiatives, so also is a political consensus that transcends partisanship. In the American context, this means the endorsement of both major political parties is necessary for a new international posture to endure. This marks the particular significance of President Dwight D. Eisenhower and his administration. As the first Republican president elected in 24 years, and who ran a campaign sharply critical of Truman's foreign policy, Eisenhower might have been expected to reject the Roosevelt-Truman model of internationalism and pluralism. Instead, Eisenhower largely embraced this worldview and succeeded in putting it on a solid bipartisan foundation so that it has endured in America for the succeeding six decades.

To do this, Eisenhower first had to bring his own party on board. His very decision to run for president as a Republican in 1952 stemmed largely from his concern over the growing influence of Senator Robert Taft's isolationist views in the party, to the point that Eisenhower entered the race primarily to block Taft from the nomination. Eisenhower pulled no rhetorical punches in criticizing isolationism and trying to expunge it from his party. In a June 1952 debate, he declared:

> Those who assert that America can live solely within its own borders, those who seem to think we have little or no stake in the rest of the world and what happens to it . . . such persons are taking an unjustified gamble with peace. They are no friends of American security. Theirs is not the counsel of enlightened self-interest. It is the counsel of eventual self-destruction. And the American people have shown time and again that they will not support this stupid and myopic doctrine. . . . The bleak scene of an America surrounded by a savage wolf pack could be our lot if we heed the false prophets of living alone.[25]

In winning over his party to robust American security commitments abroad, Eisenhower also appealed to all Americans to support their nation's global leadership role.

Secretary of State John Foster Dulles served as an eager partner in this effort. Dulles in particular deftly employed American history to make the case for American international commitments. He hearkened back to the Founding Fathers' generation to offer an internationalist interpretation of American history, and in speeches and press conferences Dulles frequently channeled Abraham Lincoln's more expansive interpretation of America's founding charter. In Dulles's words, "I have often quoted what Abraham Lincoln said about the Declaration of Independence. He said that it meant hope not alone for the people of this country, but hope for the world for all future time."[26] In another oft-cited theme, Dulles proclaimed that America's "Founders believed that men had their origins and destiny in God, that they were endowed by Him with inalienable rights, that they had responsibilities and duties prescribed by moral law, and that man's job on earth was to build the kind of a society that would help men to develop their God-given responsibilities."[27] In such ways Dulles offered his answers to the enduring debates about America's origins. He believed that as a "city on a hill" America had a mission to the world: that the Declaration's promise of human equality applied to all people in all places, and that Washington's aversion to alliances only applied to the young nation's fragile status in the late eighteenth century.

This last point found further illustration in Eisenhower and Dulles's enthusiasm for deepening America's alliances. As historian John Lewis Gaddis points out, alliances played a central role in the Eisenhower administration's strategic doctrine, as exemplified by its main strategy document NSC 162/2. This National Security Council document argued "that the United States could not 'meet its defense needs, even at exorbitant cost, without the support of allies,'" Gaddis writes, adding, "It is significant that Dulles, in his 1954 *Foreign Affairs* article, listed alliances ahead even of nuclear deterrent capability as 'the cornerstone of security for the free nations.'"[28] In specific terms, besides reaffirming their commitment to NATO, Eisenhower and Dulles also expanded America's alliance structure in Asia. This included forming the Southeast Asia Treaty Organization (SEATO) in 1954, which added Pakistan and Thailand to America's existing alliances with Australia, New Zealand, and the Philippines, as well as crafting separate bilateral treaties with South Korea in 1953 and Taiwan in 1955.

Like Truman, Eisenhower and Dulles also realized the need to lance the boil of American hypocrisy on racial and religious intolerance. A defining moment on race came in 1957 when Eisenhower took the unprecedented step of ordering National Guard troops to enforce school desegregation in Little Rock, Arkansas. Three years earlier, the U.S. Supreme Court, led by Eisenhower-appointee Chief Justice Earl Warren, issued its seminal *Brown v. Board of Education* decision declaring school segregation to violate the U.S. Constitution. Many Southern states resisted this decision, especially Governor Orville Faubus in Arkansas, and this defiance brought global opprobrium on the United States. Henry Cabot Lodge, the U.S. ambassador to the United Nations, wrote to Eisenhower that "here at the United Nations

I can see clearly the harm that the riots in Little Rock are doing to our foreign relations. More than two-thirds of the world is nonwhite and the reaction of the representatives of these people is easy to see. I suspect that we lost several votes on the Chinese communist item because of Little Rock." When Eisenhower made his speech to the nation explaining his decision to deploy National Guard troops in Arkansas, he couched it partly in terms of the Cold War:

> At a time when we face grave situations abroad because of the hatred that Communism bears toward a system of government based on human rights, it would be difficult to exaggerate the harm that is being done to the prestige and influence, and indeed to the safety, of our nation and the world. Our enemies are gloating over this incident and using it everywhere to misrepresent our whole nation. We are portrayed as a violator of those standards of conduct which the peoples of the world united to proclaim in the Charter of the United Nations.[29]

While Eisenhower, like his predecessors Roosevelt and Truman, could have done more to advance civil rights for black Americans, his intervention at Little Rock stands as a signature moment in civil rights history and established the precedent that the federal government would enforce the ideals of the Declaration of Independence and the protections of the Constitution. Eisenhower arguably made more progress in advancing religious pluralism. Part of his antipathy to communism stemmed from its militant atheism, so Eisenhower worked to forge and institutionalize more inclusive expressions of faith that brought Protestants, Catholics, and Jews together around a common belief in God. Besides his regular outreach to clergy from all faith traditions, he presided over symbolically inclusive steps such as opening his cabinet meetings in prayer, adopting "In God We Trust" as the nation's official motto and adding it to paper currency, adding the words "one Nation under God" to the Pledge of Allegiance, and establishing the annual National Prayer Breakfast. With each of these measures Eisenhower affirmed his belief in the civil equality of all faiths and his desire for his nation to be both pious and inclusive.[30]

THE PERSISTENCE OF INTERNATIONALISM
AND PLURALISM IN AMERICA

The transitions under Roosevelt, Truman, and Eisenhower were not confined to the mid-twentieth century, but have continued to evolve with each passing decade. However, in hindsight, it is clear that the three decades of these three presidencies did mark a crucial turning point in U.S. domestic and international commitments. These commitments continue to shape America's collective memory and self-identity today. For example, while differing on particular policies, almost all Americans continue to see their nation as having a responsibility of global leadership. This may seem like a truism today, but it was a deeply unpopular opinion held only by a tiny minority as recently as the 1930s. Similarly, the United States has an ongoing commitment to incorporating values into its statecraft, rather than just material interests and raison d'état. The transitions and progress made during these pivotal mid-century years have also equipped most Americans to be candid in admitting and discussing our nation's past failures, such as on civil rights or the irresponsible isolationism of the 1930s. Of course this does not mean that these issues are permanently resolved in a concrete manner. The Charleston church massacre in 2015 and ongoing debates over public displays of the Confederate flag, or disputes over America's nonintervention in Syria, are just a few recent examples of the persistence of these questions. Yet it is striking how public discussions, even over these painful issues, operate under shared assumptions. Virtually all Americans agree on racial and religious equality, and almost all agree on our nation's international leadership responsibilities; it is merely the particulars that provoke debate.

America's historical experiences and efforts to come to terms with this history might offer some potential lessons for the contemporary context. Following are a few possible insights:

- *The domestic and the international are inseparable.* It often takes external challenges to drive internal change. Geopolitical developments and crises such as the rise of Nazi Germany, Imperial Japan's attack on Pearl Harbor, the expansionist threat of Soviet communism, and the international opprobrium suffered by the United States for its racism all helped catalyze profound internal changes in American political and cultural life.
- *Political leadership is essential.* Even in the midst of these geopolitical shifts, it took courageous and visionary political leaders such as Roosevelt, Truman, and Eisenhower to lead the United States through the necessary changes. A domestic consensus rarely develops on its own organically, but needs to be forged and harnessed by political leadership.
- *Power should shape the nation's strategy.* This may sound like a truism, but it helps explain in strategic terms how and why the United States could shift from no alliances to many alliances. For a relatively weak nation, alliances can pose a threat of dragging the nation into a conflict that it is unable to handle. Whereas for a relatively strong nation, alliances can be force multipliers, displays of strength that simultaneously increase its strength and power projection. America's eschewal of alliances may have made good sense for the relatively weak nation of the nineteenth century, just as its embrace of alliances made good sense for the strong nation that emerged after World War II.
- *History can answer history.* Every nation has a complex history that mixes elements of virtue and vice and is susceptible to multiple interpretations. In seeking to come to terms with the unfavorable aspects of its past, a nation should embrace the ennobling dimensions of its past. Roosevelt, Truman, and Eisenhower all cited the founders to rebut isolationists and inspire the American people to internationalist commitments.
- *Timing informs prudence and boldness.* As audacious as each of these U.S. presidents were, each also constantly gauged the

political currents to see just how far he could go in pressing for change. Each knew that overreach, beyond what the international or domestic situation could bear, would be disastrous. Each also knew that excessive passivity and caution would lead to missed opportunities and stagnation. Prudent leadership means reading the times carefully to see when boldness is called for, and when caution is warranted.

• *Partners and institutions are indispensable.* Roosevelt, Truman, and Eisenhower were only able to succeed and make their changes endure because they enlisted political partners from the opposing party, and because they developed institutions to lock in American's international commitments and protection of civil rights long after they left office.

NOTES

1. The text of this sermon is available at http://winthropsociety.com/doc_charity.php. For more on Winthrop, see Edmund S. Morgan, *The Puritan Dilemma: The Story of John Winthrop* (New York: Longman, 1999).

2. The full text of the Declaration of Independence is available at http://www.archives.gov/exhibits/charters/declaration_transcript.html.

3. The full text of President George Washington's Farewell Address is available at https://history.state.gov/milestones/1784-1800/washington-farewell.

4. Walter MacDougall, *Promised Land, Crusader State: The American Encounter with the World since 1776* (New York: Mariner Books, 1997), 51.

5. See, for example, Robert Kagan, *Dangerous Nation: American Foreign Policy from its Earliest Days to the Dawn of the Twentieth Century* (New York: Vintage, 2007); and Max Boot, *The Savage Wars of Peace: Small Wars and the Rise of American Power* (New York: Basic Books, 2002).

6. Cited in David Kaiser, *No End Save Victory: How FDR Led the Nation into War* (New York: Basic Books, 2014), 55.

7. Cited in Michael Gerson, "1952 All Over Again," *National Journal*, June 21, 2014, http://www.nationaljournal.com/magazine/1952-all-over-again-20140618.

8. Quoted in Kaiser, *No End Save Victory*, 165–166.

9. Quoted in Gerson, "1952 All Over Again."

10. Quoted in Kaiser, *No End Save Victory*, 51.

11. Franklin D. Roosevelt, "Message to Congress Urging Repeal of the Embargo Provisions of the Neutrality Law," September 21, 1939, http://www.presidency.ucsb.edu/ws/index.php?pid=15813. Note that Kaiser also cites this speech (*No End Save Victory*, 53–54), but mistakenly dates it on September 22.

12. Elizabeth Borgwardt, *A New Deal for the World: America's Vision for Human Rights* (Cambridge, MA: Harvard University Press, 2005), 5.

13. William Inboden, "The Atlantic Charter's Enduring Relevance," *Transatlantic Take* (blog), German Marshall Fund, August 11, 2011, http://www.gmfus.org/blog /2011/08/11/atlantic-charters-enduring-relevance.

14. The full text of the Atlantic Charter is available at http://www.nato.int/cps /en/natolive/official_texts_16912.htm.

15. Kaiser, *No End Save Victory*, 231.

16. For more on the Four Chaplains and this broader theme of improving interfaith relations, see Kevin M. Schultz, *Tri-Faith America: How Catholics and Jews Held Postwar America to Its Protestant Promise* (New York: Oxford University Press, 2011).

17. Cited in Joseph Nye, *Presidential Leadership and the Creation of the American Era* (Princeton, NJ: Princeton University Press, 2013), 42.

18. See Melvyn Leffler, *A Preponderance of Power: National Security, the Truman Administration, and the Cold War* (Stanford, CA: Stanford University Press, 1992), 281.

19. Robert A. Taft, "Speech on the North Atlantic Treaty," July 26, 1949, http:// teachingamericanhistory.org/library/document/speech-on-the-north-atlantic -treaty/.

20. Quoted in William Inboden, *Religion and American Foreign Policy, 1945–1960: The Soul of Containment* (New York: Cambridge University Press, 2010), 105.

21. Nye, *Presidential Leadership*, 41.

22. Mary Dudziak, *Cold War Civil Rights: Race and the Image of American Democracy* (Princeton, NJ: Princeton University Press, 2000), 27.

23. Quoted in ibid., 82.

24. For more on this initiative, see Inboden, *Religion and American Foreign Policy*.

25. Quoted in Gerson, "1952 All Over Again."

26. Quoted in Jonathan Nashel, *Edward Lansdale's Cold War* (Amherst: University of Massachusetts Press, 2005), 246.

27. Quoted in Inboden, *Religion and American Foreign Policy*, 234.

28. John Lewis Gaddis, *Strategies of Containment: A Critical Appraisal of American National Security Policy during the Cold War* (New York: Oxford University Press, 2005), 149–150.

29. Lodge and Eisenhower quotes both in Dudziak, *Cold War Civil Rights*, 131, 133.

30. For more on Eisenhower's religious devotion and pluralism, see Inboden, *Religion and American Foreign Policy*, 257–309.

3. JAPAN IN THE GLOBAL HISTORY OF THE TWENTIETH CENTURY: A PATH TO "PROACTIVE CONTRIBUTION TO PEACE"

Shinichi Kitaoka and Yuichi Hosoya

No other major powers experienced as turbulent a history in the twentieth century as Japan. Japan won the Russo-Japanese War in the beginning of the twentieth century, but it was unthinkable then that a non-Western power could defeat one of the most powerful Western nations. Japan then participated in the Council of Ten at the Paris Peace Conference, as one of the five victorious powers in the First World War. In 1920 Japan became one of the four permanent members to the Council within the League of Nations.

However, during the Second World War, Japan had become the enemy of the Allied powers and fought a war against the United States and the United Kingdom, and then the Soviet Union. Japan decided to challenge the international order, and damaged it significantly. In September 1951, Japan's prime minister, Shigeru Yoshida, signed the U.S.-Japan security treaty that turned Japan from a former enemy to an indispensable ally of the United States during the Cold War years.

What are the lessons that we should draw from Japan's experiences in the twentieth century? How should we view Japan's path in the global history of the twentieth century? To answer these questions, on February 25, 2015, Prime Minister Shinzo Abe organized the "Advisory Panel on the History of the 20th Century and on Japan's Role and the World Order in the 21st Century."

After five months of discussion, the Advisory Panel submitted its final report to Prime Minister Abe. This report became an important basis for Abe's statement, issued on August 14, 2015, on the 70th anniversary of the end of World War II.[1] The report summarized the path of Japan in the twentieth century by stating that:

> In the first half of the twentieth century, Japan was still a poor, largely agricultural country, and the idea came to prevail in the 1930s that development would be secured by territorial expansion instead of building wealth through industry and trade. The political system in pre-war Japan was also flawed.[2]

The report continues:

> However, in the second half of the twentieth century, based on deep remorse over the war, Japan has been reborn as a country that is completely different from what it was in the first half of the twentieth century, particularly in the period between the 1930s and the first half of the 1940s. Peace, rule of law, liberal democracy, respect for human rights, the free trade system, self-determination, support for the economic development of developing countries, etc. are what characterize post-war Japan.[3]

Much of the Japanese media seemed to share the view of Japan's path in the twentieth century as described in the final report of the Advisory Panel.[4] Based on this understanding, Prime Minister Abe presented a balanced statement on the 70th anniversary of the end of the Second World War evaluated by many foreign governments and in media commentaries.[5] Abe's statement arguably reflected a national consensus on historical understandings of Japan's path in the twentieth century.

While Abe's statement has political and diplomatic implications, it is important to reflect on the path of Japan in the global history of the twentieth century from a historian's perspective.

FROM THE NINETEENTH CENTURY TO
THE TWENTIETH CENTURY

Gordon Martel, a professor of history at the University of Northern British Columbia, described the features of twentieth-century international history as follows: "The international history of the twentieth century is best understood as one of imperial struggle in which states—usually calling themselves nations—sought to impress their own version of modernity and progress on the world."[6] He continues: "The Great Powers of the world in 1900 consisted of Britain, France, Russia, and the United States; each believed in a destiny unique to itself, and each believed that this destiny could be realized only through the assertion of power over vast tracts of territory."[7]

Based on a similar assessment of the international environment at that time, Joseph Chamberlain, Britain's colonial secretary from 1895 to 1903, declared that "the days are for great Empires and not for little States."[8] Likewise, Herbert Asquith, British prime minister in 1914, described territorial expansion as "normal, as necessary, as inescapable and unmistakably a sign of vitality in a nation as the corresponding processes in the growing human body."[9]

The early twentieth century thus featured the expansion of European imperialism on a global scale. Japan and the United States, two non-European great powers, joined this imperial struggle in their own ways. The European imperial struggle became a global imperial struggle. To put it simply, as Martel wrote: "Every great power before 1914 was an empire either in name or in practice."[10] Similarly, John Darwin, an imperial historian at Oxford, wrote:

> To an extent inconceivable as late as 1860, the world of 1900 was an imperial world: of territorial empires spreading across much of the globe; and of informal empires of trade, unequal treaties and extraterritorial privilege (for Europeans)—and garrisons and gunboats to enforce it—over most of the rest.[11]

In the nineteenth century, colonization by European empires had spread around the world thanks to Western technological innovations in transportation, communications, and military power. With their military superiority based on this technological innovation, the great powers in Europe could easily control territories outside the European continent. In other words, it was a period when might was stronger than right in a Hobbesian sense. Japan had become the first non-Western great power that could join in this imperial rivalry.[12] More precisely, as historian W. G. Beasley noted, "Japanese imperialism becomes the illegitimate child of *Western* capitalism, with international rivalry as midwife."[13]

China was the most powerful country in the world for centuries in global history and remained the world's most prosperous country until as late as the 1830s. China's defeat at the hands of British military power in the two Opium Wars, which the Chinese people considered an inhumane and unjust assault on China's empire and civilization, shocked the international system and introduced a period of Western imperialism in Asia.

By the end of the nineteenth century, the United States, despite the fact that it had been a former colonial territory of the British Empire and had advocated an anticolonial ideology, occupied the Philippines after the Spanish-American War. Furthermore, the murder of two missionaries in China gave Germany, which did not have much to do with Asian affairs until then, a reason to occupy and lease Jiaozhou Bay, which then led to the widening of Germany's sphere of influence over the entire Shandong Province, a huge area home to 100 million people today.

The Meiji Restoration was the significant break from Japan's previous place in international society, as Japan had closed its society from the outside world. Since the Meiji Restoration, Japan decided to participate in Western international society where imperialism was a major trend among great powers. Japan had been pursuing modernization during this period of European imperialism to avoid colonization, and Japan fought a war against the Qing dynasty and occupied Taiwan. The Sino-Japanese War of 1894–1895 was Japan's first experience in modern warfare and marked its emergence as an expansionist power. In other words, Japan adapted to the tide of European imperialism and acquired its own colonial territories.[14]

THE RUSSO-JAPANESE WAR AS A TURNING POINT

The wave of Western imperialism in the nineteenth century would inevitably invite a backlash, and the decolonization movement followed. The Russo-Japanese War of 1904–1905 had a major impact in this regard. Japan's victory in the war aroused revolutionary fervor in various countries oppressed by Russia, such as Finland, Poland, and Turkey. Rotem Kowner, a professor of Japanese history at the University of Haifa, underlined the importance of the psychological impact of the Russo-Japanese War on the trajectory of global history: "Colonial subjects across the world—from Southeast Asia and the Indian subcontinent to the Middle East—were all thrilled by the war."[15] Kowner also wrote:

> With such a mindset nationalist and revolutionary ideas could thrive in the hope of future realization. During the war new sectors of the colonial population, Asia in particular, began to share their distress over the foreign rule and manifest a desire for a national self-definition. More radical segments of this population viewed the victory of Japan, a developing Asian country, over a major European power as a symbol, and as a portent for their own prospects of breaking free of colonial rule and taking the course of modernization on the Japanese model.[16]

Those who heard of Japan's victory over Russia in their childhood, or those who heard it from their parents, subsequently rose up for the independence of colonies in Asia and Africa after World War I. In this sense, the Russo-Japanese War initiated a major movement of global decolonization.

Less than 10 years later a conflict emerged among the great powers in Europe, leading to the outbreak of World War I. The war resulted in a major, revolutionary change in the world order. Thus, as Michael Howard, a famous British historian of the war, wrote,

"The United States, now the most powerful nation in the world, was liberal democracy incarnate, and its leader, President Woodrow Wilson, had a clear perception of the new world order he intended to introduce together with the power to impose it."[17]

Meanwhile, noble dynasties on the European continent such as the Romanov, Habsburg, and Hohenzollern collapsed, leading to a period of great transformation. A movement of ethnic self-determination then emerged. While this movement did not include Asia, it inevitably had a major influence on the region as evidenced by the May Fourth Movement in China and the March First Movement in Korea. The great powers would be forced to respond to the rise of nationalism around the world.

World War I was probably the most inhumane war in terms of carnage. The death toll was higher in World War II, yet considering the battlefields alone, World War I was an extremely horrific war with huge numbers of casualties. As a result, efforts to declare war illegal as an instrument of national policy progressed. Articles that required countries not to resort to war were included in the Covenant of the League of Nations; the Kellogg-Briand Pact or Paris Peace Pact, concluded in 1928, renounced war as an instrument of national policy and created a new norm of internationalism, though it did not include any enforcement provisions.[18]

On September 10, 1931, Robert Cecil, a leading British politician, addressed the Assembly of the League of Nations as follows:

> I do not think that there is any prospect of any war. I know ... how rash it is to prophesy as to the future of international affairs; but, nevertheless, I do not believe that there is anyone in this room who will contradict me when I say that there has scarcely ever been a period in the world's history when war seems less likely than it does at the present.[19]

Barely a week later, an incident in Manchuria sparked one of the most unstable and confrontational periods in international history. Robert Cecil did not notice that Japan's Kwantung Army was preparing a military offensive in Northern China.

THE FAILURE TO GUARANTEE STABILITY AND PEACE

Why was the period from 1925 until 1931 relatively stable, and why did it fail to remain so? Several important international agreements existed among the great powers during this period to maintain the status quo. Even though the new norm of national self-determination was widely welcomed, the great powers did not intend to abandon their own colonial territories. Similarly, the Paris Peace Pact did not include any clauses to enforce the norms it espoused. The United States underwrote stability in this period as a model of liberal democracy and prosperity that sustained the world order. The strength of the U.S. economy supported the reparations of Germany and other countries, and the same applied in Asia as well. Trade with the United States also buoyed the Japanese economy in the 1920s. Under such circumstances, the principle of economic development—in other words, the belief that the international order could be maintained if the economy continued to develop—became popular.

This system subsequently collapsed, however, and several factors explain this upheaval of the international order. For example, the anti-imperialism movement, or activities of the colonies to gain independence, became extremely radical in large part due to the influence of the Soviet Union. Another factor was the return of the Soviet Union as a strong military power that challenged international harmony as a whole and changed the balance of international politics. Above all, the Great Depression decimated the global economy as well as the idealistic notion that economic development alone was a recipe for stability. This development sent shockwaves throughout Europe and affected Japan severely.

In this context, totalitarianism emerged as a model in Turkey, Italy, the Soviet Union, and Germany, replacing American democracy as the standard-bearer for world order. Countries dismissed the principle of economic development, and ideas such as autarky and *Lebensraum* (living space) emerged. Visions of democratic governance as a foundation for economic prosperity gave way to an ideology touting territorial expansion and military power as the keys to survival, which Japan ultimately adopted.

Reflecting on the global history of the twentieth century, we see that Japan lost sight of international trends that existed in the world until then, such as the backlash against colonization, the desire to proscribe war through peace treaties, and a belief in the principle of economic development as an anchor of stability. Japan waged a reckless war that took a heavy toll on human life, especially in Asia, and sent many of its soldiers to battlefields without adequate supplies and weapons, letting them die. Ordinary Japanese citizens also suffered through air raids that damaged infrastructure and quality of life. Japan did not pay heed to the trend of decolonization either, and in the late 1930s in particular, its rule over the colonies became increasingly harsh. Considering these points, we must declare that the government and military leaders of Japan in and after the 1930s bear heavy responsibility. Additionally, it is difficult to confirm the fact that Japan fought for the liberation of Asia, although many Asian countries gained independence as a result of the war Japan conducted from the 1930s to 1945. Japan made many decisions deemed critical for its own survival and self-defense—though the rationale was wrong—and few were for the liberation of Asia. While some people did genuinely fight to liberate Asia, we believe it is incorrect to argue that Japan fought for that purpose.

WHY DID JAPAN TURN TO MILITARISM?

It is necessary to examine why Japan embarked on such a course toward military expansionism.[20] First, we should remember that Japan was a poor, agrarian country in the years before World War II. Ordinary citizens as well as the armed forces shared a strong desire to acquire more land and territory based on the belief that Japan lacked resources and should seek them abroad or that it should seek external markets because the domestic market was too small.

Some argued that, from a geopolitical and strategic point of view, Japan should secure its front for fear of future military expansion by the Soviet Union. The argument for expansion also rested on the notion that Japan lacked the space to absorb its population, which was increasing rapidly at the time, unlike now. A perceived link between territorial expansion and the honor of the nation further stimulated the debate. Of course, some held different views, as exemplified by Tanzan Ishibashi, who argued in the 1910s that Japan should exist as a trading state but considered territorial expansion irrational.[21] This did not become the majority view, however.

Taisho democracy thrived in many respects for a nation that had only established its own constitution 40 years earlier, but the institutions that underpinned it were weak indeed, particularly compared with the authorities available to the military. Thus, the weakness of the prime minister's power was another factor that contributed to the gradual rise of militarism in Japanese politics. The Meiji Constitution of 1889 created a very fragile political system in prewar Japan. The military was not under the prime minister's command and could maintain a high level of autonomy within Japan's political system without strong interference. Hence, it was very difficult for any prime minister to control effectively the Kwantung Army when it invaded Manchuria.[22]

Limited freedom of speech, which caused serious problems in Japan's external policy, also contributed to the rise of militarism. This became particularly significant after the second Sino-Japanese War escalated in 1937. In contrast, a degree of free speech existed in 1931 when the Manchurian Incident occurred and intellectuals as well as journalists often criticized the behavior of the Kwantung Army. Tighter controls were instituted at the outbreak of the Sino-Japanese War in 1937 and that changed the atmosphere considerably. Japanese society became more subservient to the military and it became impossible to criticize its actions.

Furthermore, the Japanese military authorities were extremely self-righteous and criticized subsequent sanctions against Japan by the international community. Military leaders thought they did nothing wrong and argued Japan should be more confrontational toward countries that sought to obstruct their activities.

JAPAN IN THE LIBERAL INTERNATIONAL ORDER

Unlike the tumult of the 1930s, the conditions for stability and prosperity in the years after World War II were very firmly established based on rules and norms that governed the postwar liberal international order.

First, in the post–World War II world, the prohibition of the use of military force as a means to settle international disputes has become a norm through instruments such as Article 2 of the Charter of the United Nations. With its "peace" constitution of 1947, Japan has become the country that is, so to speak, the most faithful to this norm. The first paragraph under Article 9 of the Constitution of Japan prescribes the norm as follows: "Aspiring sincerely to an international peace based on justice and order, the Japanese people forever renounce war as a sovereign right of the nation and the threat or use of force as means of settling international disputes."[23]

Second, the development of the free-trade system after the Second World War facilitated Japan's postwar economic growth. Japan abandoned its legacy of autarky and could purchase natural resources and export its products freely without any military expansion by force. The factors that contributed to prewar military expansionism were no longer relevant, and an overwhelming majority in contemporary Japan believes that Japan can prosper through international trade and integration with the global economy.

Third, the prime minister has more power under the parliamentary cabinet system and the constitution guarantees freedom of speech. In addition, the United Nations has a much stronger system of enforcing sanctions, and if Japan were to become subject to international economic sanctions (though that kind of situation is improbable), it would become helplessly vulnerable. Hence, we can state with assurance that, in view of the basic conditions that support the prosperity of contemporary Japan, it would never turn its back on the international community and pursue expansionism as it did in the period before World War II.

THE CHALLENGES FOR THE FUTURE

What are the challenges Japan will face in the future? Based on Japan's experience in the twentieth century, it appears that the most critical challenge is to maintain an international order based on political freedom and an open economic architecture regionally and globally. The current government under Prime Minister Shinzo Abe has argued that Japan will continually benefit from free trade and entered the Trans-Pacific Partnership (TPP) trade negotiations toward that end. Abe also introduced Japan's first national security strategy in 2013 focused on upholding international norms such as democracy, the rule of law, human rights, and the peaceful settlement of disputes.[24] Japan's near-term strategic trajectory therefore favors an increased leadership role in preserving the international order that paved the way for Japan's remarkable postwar development in the middle of the twentieth century.

However, Japan should not choose the path of "one-country pacifism" focused on domestic prosperity without caring about peace in the rest of the world. Japan should play a more constructive role in the international community in the twenty-first century. To do so, it will be important for Japan to enhance its contributions to international security by developing its own defense capabilities and strengthening the Japan-U.S. alliance for the stability of East Asia as a whole. In sum, Japan should become a provider, not just a beneficiary, of public goods that support stability in the international system. From this perspective, we can understand that the principle of "Proactive Contribution to Peace," a cornerstone of the Abe government's national security strategy, is based on lessons Japan learned from twentieth-century international history. In the face of multiple challenges threatening to undermine the world order, Japan should collaborate with the United States and other like-minded countries to create a common set of principles that will underwrite global peace and prosperity for the twenty-first century and beyond.

NOTES

1. Statement by Prime Minister Shinzo Abe, August 14, 2015, http://japan.kantei .go.jp/97_abe/statement/201508/0814statement.html.

2. *Report of the Advisory Panel on the History of the 20th Century and on Japan's Role and the World Order in the 21st Century*, Tokyo, August 6, 2015, 5–6, http://www.kantei .go.jp/jp/singi/21c_koso/pdf/report_en.pdf.

3. Ibid.

4. For reactions to the advisory panel report, see, for example, Yasuaki Onuma, "Senso no hansei sekai ni shimeshite" [Presenting Historical Reflections to the World], *Yomiuri Shimbun*, August 7, 2015; Makoto Iokibe, "Kako to genzai, seijuku-sita ninshiki," *Mainichi Shimbun*, August 7, 2015; Editorial, "Wakai heno messeiji wo," *Asahi Shimbun*, August, 7, 2015; "Yottsu no kiiwado moura," *Nikkei Shimbun*, August 14, 2015. All four major Japanese newspapers presented positive reactions to the report of the Advisory Panel. However, *Asahi Shimbun* was critical of Abe's statement of August 14, 2015, while agreeing with the basic arguments of the report. See Editorial, "Nanno tame ni dashitanoka," *Asahi Shimbun*, August 15, 2015. Among the four major daily newspapers in Japan, *Asahi* was the only one that strongly criticized the argument in Abe's statement.

5. See, for example, "Asia Should Focus More on the Future than the Past," *Financial Times*, August 17, 2015; Jennifer Lind, "Shinzo Abe's Balancing Act," *Wall Street Journal*, August 20, 2015; Daniel Twining, "Why Is China Still Dredging Up the Ghost of Imperial Japan?," *Foreign Policy*, September 1, 2015; "Rekishi no kyokun mune ni mirai wo hirakou" [Let Us Open the Future by Reflecting on the Lessons of History], *Yomiuri Shimbun*, August 15, 2015; "70 nen danwa wo fumae nani wo suruka da" [With the Statement on the 70th Anniversary of the End of the War in Mind, the Question Is What to Do], *Nikkei Shimbun*, August 15, 2015. Some media sources presented rather critical comments on Abe's statement. For example, see Howard W. French, "Abe's Avoidance of the Past," *New York Times*, August 18, 2015.

6. Gordon Martel, "Twentieth-Century International History: The Changing Face of Empire," in *A Companion to International History 1900–2001*, ed. Gordon Martel (London: Blackwell, 2007), 3.

7. Ibid.

8. Quoted in ibid., 4.

9. Ibid.

10. Ibid.

11. John Darwin, *After Tamerlane: The Rise and Fall of Global Empires, 1400–2000* (London: Penguin, 2008), 288–289.

12. On Japan's entry into European international society, see Hidemi Suganami, "Japan's Entry into International Society," in *The Expansion of International Society*, ed. Hedley Bull and Adam Watson (Oxford: Oxford University Press, 1984), 185–199.

13. W. G. Beasley, *Japanese Imperialism 1894–1945* (Oxford: Oxford University Press, 1987), 9.

14. On Japan's approach to colonialism, see Mark R. Peattie, "Japanese Attitudes toward Colonialism, 1895–1945," in *The Japanese Colonial Empire, 1895–1945*, ed. Ramon H. Myers and Mark R. Peattie (Princeton, NJ: Princeton University Press, 1984), 80–127.

15. Rotem Kowner, "Between a Colonial Clash and World War Zero: The Impact of the Russo-Japanese War in a Global Perspective," in *The Impact of the Russo-Japanese War*, ed. Rotem Kowner (New York: Routledge, 2007), 19.

16. Ibid.

17. Michael Howard, *The Invention of Peace: Reflections on War and International Order* (New Haven, CT: Yale University Press, 2000), 61.

18. Andrew Webster, "Internationalism," in Martel, *Companion to International History*, 43.

19. Quoted in Martyn Housden, *The League of Nations and the Organisation of Peace* (London: Longman, 2012), 98.

20. On the transformation of Japanese domestic politics and society, see Shin-ichi Kitaoka, *Seito kara gunbu he: Nihon no kindai* [From Party Politics toward the Military: Modern Japan], 1924–1941 (Tokyo: Chuokoronshinsha, 2013), 5:151–285.

21. On the philosophy of Tanzan Ishibashi, see, for example, "Ishibashi Tanzan: A Liberal Business Journalist," in *Sources of Japanese Tradition: Volume Two: 1600 to 2000, Part Two: 1868 to 2000*, ed. Wm. Theodore de Bary, Carol Gluck, and Arthur E. Tiedemann (New York: Columbia University Press, 2006), 181–189.

22. Makoto Iokibe, "Introduction: Japanese Diplomacy from Prewar to Postwar," in *The Diplomatic History of Postwar Japan*, ed. Makoto Iokibe, trans. Robert D. Eldridge (London: Routledge, 2011), 6–7.

23. The full text of the Constitution of Japan is available at http://japan.kantei .go.jp/constitution_and_government_of_japan/constitution_e.html.

24. "National Security Strategy of Japan," Cabinet Secretariat, Tokyo, December 17, 2013, http://www.cas.go.jp/jp/siryou/131217anzenhoshou/nss-e.pdf.

4. THE TURKISH EXPERIENCE OF THE TWENTIETH CENTURY

Cemil Aydin

THE 1980S MODERNITY DEBATE ON THE NATURE OF TWENTIETH-CENTURY WORLD HISTORY

During my college years in the late 1980s, there was a debate on modernism and postmodernism in Istanbul cafes and classrooms. This was principally a reflection about how to interpret the evolution of twentieth-century world history. Was this a century of humanity's emancipation, progress and welfare, and improvements in international justice, or was this a century of racism, dehumanization, genocides and subjugation of human beings, and oppressive bureaucratic rationality of various modern states?

Retrospectively, there were many positive aspects of twentieth-century history. Rising living standards, better diet, control of diseases, empowerment of women in many societies, increasing human mobility, and educational opportunities are just some of the diffused achievements of humanity in the twentieth century. Part of the reason for higher living standards was urbanization, where big cities then allowed a majority of human beings to have access to electricity, sanitation, roads and other transit systems, refrigerators and washing machines in homes, as well as television sets and other forms of middle-class entertainment. Although the twentieth century witnessed an improvement in the quality of life for many of world's populations, it had moments, events, processes, and periods marked by wars and mass killing, producing millions of shattered lives.

My professors in the Department of Political Science, History, and Sociology at Boğaziçi University made us read about the major global debates on twentieth-century modernity, exposing us to writers from Martin Heidegger to Michel Foucault. In the battle over moral narratives of the twentieth century in Europe, a group of critical intellectuals underlined the darker aspects of the modern century, symbolized by the horrors of World War II such as the Holocaust.[1] These intellectuals questioned the utopias of enlightenment, modernization, justice, and liberty, by showing how the evils of the twentieth century such as mass political violence, authoritarianism, racism, colonialism, environmental destruction, and multiple other forms of human suffering are linked essentially to processes and ideas described as modern and enlightened. Some of these intellectuals were recommending that we should free ourselves from the assumption and promises of the nineteenth-century ideals of progress, enlightenment, and modernity, or the notion of Western superiority, which were all guilty of these dark sides of the twentieth century.[2]

In response, there were intellectuals, such as German social theorist Jurgen Habermas, who conceded the dark episodes and aspects of the twentieth century but insisted that Eurocentric modernist projects can learn from past failures and there was no reason to throw out the baby with the bathwater. In one of his autobiographical writings, Habermas noted how, as a young West German citizen listening to the Nuremberg trials on the radio and hearing about many atrocities committed by the German government, he would reflect on why German society that gave birth to humanist philosophers like Immanuel Kant could also give rise to Nazism and Hitler. He believed that we could learn from the mistakes and negative developments of the modern century to recommit ourselves to future promises of emancipation and justice.[3]

This European as well as global debate on modernism, antimodernism, and postmodernism in the last decade of the Cold War represents the core question about the moral story of the twentieth-century world: How is it that, on the one hand, the twentieth century was a dark century of dehumanization, domination of humans by totalitarian state structures, and systematic and mass cruelty by human beings against other humans,[4] while on the other hand, it was also a century when some of the possibilities of human freedom and empowerment were actually realized? It was better to be a woman at the end of the twentieth century than at the beginning of it. A majority of human beings on this earth in the early twentieth century was ruled by European colonial empires, while by the end of the century they gained the dignity of national self-determination. As historians of subaltern studies have shown, national independence did not mean the end of all kinds of exploitation, violence, and discrimination, and average people could be oppressed by people of their own nation and race in the postcolonial period. Yet national independence became a first step to create conditions for better life for billions of people, as the stories of India and China best exemplify today. The eventual denunciation of racism and colonialism, the rise of human rights as a collective global ideal and of the welfare state and internationalism, worldwide improvements in public health, education and literacy, and human beings' mastery over nature via the progress of science and technology could also be mentioned as positive achievements of the century.[5]

Scholarship on twentieth-century modernity heavily relied on the European experience: Europe's promise of a utopian century seemed to be averted by two world wars (inter-Europe civil wars), anti-Semitism, the Holocaust, and Nazism and Stalinism, but eventually arrived as the end of history in today's European Union. Postwar Europe remained peaceful despite the Cold War division of the continent. With the end of the Cold War, there is a sense of triumph of European exceptionalism that out of all regions of the world, Europe was most successful in terms of economic prosperity and standards of good governance. This Eurocentric triumphalist story of the peaceful half century after 1945 faced critiques about Europe's complicity and promotion of wars in other regions, such as the violence and suffering it caused in Algeria, Vietnam, and South Asia, and even on its own continent in Bosnia in the 1990s. Europe's self-congratulatory narratives avoid a necessary conversation on economic exploitation, discriminatory policies against minorities, and Europe's perpetuation of an unjust international order. Europe's denial of its colonial past and its Islamophobia encourages other nations to follow similar paths of mass violence and often express a comparison with Europe: If white Europeans can get away with their denial of past crimes of colonialism and imperialism, why should other societies face them? Yet, whatever Europe's imperfections, the success of the European Union gave twentieth-century modernist promises of a better life a new form and geopolitical content.

As a student of sociology and history in the late 1980s in Istanbul, I was following this global debate on the meaning of the modern century against the background of struggles with democratization in Turkey, the intense debate on Turkish history, and the chaotic developments in Turkey's region. As a country in the borderlands between Europe and Asia, or Christian Europe and the Islamicate societies, Turkish political and intellectual life has been shaped by competing narratives of the twentieth century. In many instances, Turkey tried to reconcile or synthesize multiple Muslim, Asian, European, or socialist/capitalist perspectives of the global order of the twentieth century. Turkey was part of a cosmopolitan empire at the beginning of the twentieth century, an empire that included large Arab, Greek, and Armenian populations, geographically extending even to North Africa. After a set of tragic events from 1911 to 1923, especially the experience of World War I, this empire became smaller in size and ethnically limited to Muslim Turks and Kurds, and transformed into a republic in 1923. Then, the new Republic of Turkey tried to establish a secular Turkish nation, suppressing public expressions of Islamic and Kurdish identity. Turkey almost converted from Eastern to Western civilization and, in that process, defeated the image of the "terrible Turk" dominant in Western public opinion.[6] By the 1950s, in the context of the Cold War, Walter Cronkite aired an American television documentary titled "The Incredible Turk," praising the achievements of President Mustafa Kemal Atatürk and the Turkish Republic in creating a modern nation-state.[7]

Yet there were many victims of Turkey's success story, and from the 1930s to the 1990s, all the oppressed citizens of Turkish nationalism and secularism found ways to voice their objections and demand their rights. In the 1980s, part of the Kurdish population even started a guerrilla campaign, challenging the official ideology of ethnic Turkish nationalism. In the late 1980s, Turkey was just coming out of a period where an American- and European-supported military regime practiced torture in prisons, other forms of human rights abuses and persecution, and generally systemic examples of ineffective and oppressive governance. Economically, Turkey in the late 1980s was still an underdeveloped country with mass poverty, far from the G20 (Group of 20 Biggest Economies) member it is today. In short, there were many reasons why scholars and students in Istanbul would be sympathetic to a negative evaluation of twentieth-century modernity and to antimodernist intellectuals.[8]

It was in the context of the 1980s, a horrible decade in Turkish history (and the history of the whole region), that Turkey renewed its application to become a member of the European Union (EU), which excited the broader pro-democracy segments of Turkish society. Turkey's 1989 application to the European Union seemed like an affirmation of the normative, enlightened, modern values identified with Europe. The educated public hoped that an EU membership application would strengthen Turkey's democratization and accelerate economic development. There may have been many failures and dark sides of the twentieth-century Turkish experience, but this did not mean the abandonment of hope for a better future for the general public and political elites. For many Turkish citizens in the 1980s, Europe symbolized the ideals of modern good governance, human rights, democracy, and economic welfare. There were millions of Turkish guest workers in Europe at that time, spreading the "dream" of the European welfare society and good governance among all segments of Turkish society. In that context, the majority of the Turkish public's future vision had a positive role model in the European Union, although there were strong dissenting opinions within Turkey about the desirability of Turkey's inclusion in the European Union. Meanwhile, the United States, as Turkey's NATO ally, was also presenting another model of twentieth-century modernization that was perhaps less normative and idealistic compared to the European model, but still promised material benefits identified with a capitalist economy and mass consumption culture.

The last decade of the Cold War as well as the post–Cold War period of the 1990s witnessed various international episodes of violence in Turkey's neighborhood: the Iran-Iraq War; the Lebanese civil war and Israeli invasion of Lebanon; the use of chemical weapons against the Kurdish city of Halabja by Saddam Hussein's Iraqi army; the Iraqi invasion of Kuwait and subsequent first Gulf War; and genocide in Bosnia. Thus, Turkish university students or Turkish public intellectuals debating the legacies of twentieth-century modernity, globally and locally, had a more negative outlook of modernity and international order than the Turkish government pursuing the EU membership application. It was very hard to believe in a narrative of an enlightened and modern twentieth century when the United Nations and the international community was simply watching the genocide of Bosnian Muslims, or Rwandans in the early 1990s, unable to save lives. Similarly, we all knew the complicity of European governments and the United States in promoting violence in the Middle East via their proxies. Even the most ardent admirers of American or European leadership would note that it was partly American and European policies in the Middle East that eventually shattered the lives of Palestinians over three generations, or it was Europe's prejudice against Muslims that encouraged Serbian nationalists to commit mass murder against Bosnians. Similarly, white powers in Africa were complicit in the Rwandan genocide. Thus, the modernity debate of 1980s Europe seemed very Eurocentric in the sense that even very critical European intellectuals were not very concerned about the dark sides and legacies of Europe's hegemony in Asia and Africa.

In addition to intense discussions within Turkey about aligning its destiny with a European project, there were also debates within Europe about Turkey's application, which raised questions about Islam and European modernity, specifically the presence of Muslim minorities within Europe. European leaders often insisted that Turkey had not fulfilled Europe's high standards of civilization and democracy and its application to EU membership should never be accepted. Beyond discussions of technical standards and criteria for EU membership, there have been clear cultural and religious prejudices against Turkey, as Eastern European countries with lower economic and democratic standards were already EU members by the early twenty-first century while Muslim majority Turkey still is not. With these concerns in mind, a group of Turkish politicians and intellectuals hoped to identify universal values about good governance and human rights in Muslim or Asian intellectual traditions, believing that Eurocentric models of modernity were insufficient and misguided as a model for Turkish society.[9]

When I was ready to start my master's and doctoral work in 1992, I wanted to find out, academically, why modern Turkey is so obsessed about judging its progress and modernization in relation to Europe's condition, and what the non-European, especially Asian and Muslim, experience of enlightenment and modernity was about. Turkish academics as well as the general public did not pay much attention to the stories of India and China, or Asia in general. There had been an admiration for Meiji Japan in the late Ottoman period and during the 1980s, but this partial interest in Japan did not come with a curiosity about the twentieth-century experience in Asia and Africa.

While I became a scholar of world history in the last two decades, the Turkish Republic's outlook improved visibly after a very low point with an economic, political, and democratic crisis in the late 1990s. Due partly to support from European imagination and partly to the dynamism of Turkish society, Turkey became more democratic and more prosperous in the first decade of the twenty-first century. In that process, Turkey benefited greatly from the globalization of its economy and its geostrategic location, trading with postcommunist Russia, Central Asian countries, and booming Arab Gulf economies, as well as with its main trading partner, the European Union. Today, Turkey is one of the most economically dynamic nations in West Asia as well as in Southeast Europe, with universal levels of literacy, state-funded free public education (including higher education) and free, high-quality health care for all citizens. Women in Turkey have already achieved tremendous gains and freedoms, although there is much more to accomplish in the face of patriarchal traditions. On average, the large middle class in Turkey live in better homes, drive good cars, enjoy beach vacations during the summer, and purchase international brands of luxury goods. Turkey has more shopping malls than Japan or Germany, a mysterious phenomenon that also tells us about the cultural habits of frequenting these malls as a leisure activity. Turkish cities have much improved municipal services, and every city in Turkey has now been interconnected to a network of good quality highways. In addition to being the sixth most popular tourist destination in the world, Turkey also exports its culture overseas with the recent popularity of its television dramas internationally. Turkish citizens use airplanes more often in their domestic and international travel, making Turkish Airlines one of the biggest carriers in the world. The Turkish government in the first decade of the 21st century created a kind of modest welfare state with many different forms of aid for its poor citizens, making sure all basic needs are covered and effectively eliminating extreme forms of poverty.

Turkey's economic boom in the last decade occurred according to the logic of the neoliberal free-market process but also produced a series of problems in the big urban areas. The crisis of public living spaces in big cities led to the popularity and appeal of the Gezi Park protests in the summer of 2013, which began as a protest against the demolition of a park but developed into a protest against the government. The Gezi protests expressed discontent about the structural deficiencies of government after decade-long economic growth under the ruling AKP Party (Justice and Development Party). While critical of the existing government, the Gezi movement was future-oriented and sought to avoid a return to bad governance from earlier periods in twentieth-century Turkey.

In spring 2013, on the eve of the 90th anniversary of the foundation of the Turkish Republic, a retrospective evaluation of Turkey's twentieth century may have looked more positive. The recovery of the Turkish economy and normalization of its democracy came with a renewed sense of confidence that Turkey can be a regional and global actor. The Turkish state was offering one of the highest levels of international aid in the world and hosted millions of refugees from Syria. Despite attempts by official and unofficial circles in Turkey to deny the past wrongdoings of the Turkish and Ottoman state against Armenian, Kurdish, Alevi, Sunni, or Greek citizens throughout the twentieth century, there has been an increasingly confident and articulate public debate on all of these issues, with brave and persistent voices asking the state to recognize the sufferings of its victims. Thus, the more economically successful and democratic Turkey became in the first decade of the twenty-first century, the freer it became in allowing critiques of the past and present policies of the Turkish state. Major issues of historical memory, including the Armenian genocide during World War II and violence against Kurds, has been increasingly recognized and debated freely more than ever, enabling partial government policy changes in terms of recognition and reconciliation. Turkey remained an official member candidate for the European Union but no longer had an inferiority complex in relation to EU member countries. In fact, for about a decade, there was a sense that the economy and standard of living in Turkey should not be a serious obstacle to Turkey's EU membership. There were many areas where Turkey might need constitutional amendments, economic improvements, and stronger governance, but it was no longer considered a developing country.

While a new positive narrative of Turkish democracy and modernity emerged in early 2013, when the Turkish government initiated a peace-oriented dialogue with the leaders of the formerly separatist Kurdish political movement, developments in the years since then have given rise to new disillusionments about Turkish democracy and the pathologies in the structural foundations of its political modernity. A series of political and economic crises in Turkey during the past three years have illustrated the precariousness of its earlier achievements. Turkey still has a relatively functioning pluralist democracy, vibrant civil society, and prosperous economy, but there are doubts and discontent about the fairness of its constitutional system and its ability to create an inclusive and peaceful political community. The rise of armed conflicts in Eastern Turkey against Kurdish militias, coupled with eruptions of domestically and internationally linked terrorism since the summer of 2015, indicate that peace and stability associated with a pluralist democracy has not yet been achieved. The Turkish government's counterinsurgency measures against terrorist groups in some of the Kurdish majority towns resulted in the utter destruction of civilian life in those regions. More important, it became clear that Turkey could never have a single moral narrative regarding its political modernity and the legacies of its twentieth-century experience. The Turkish public was shocked by the coup attempt in July 2016, which revealed that despite all of Turkey's political and economic achievements there were still military officials and civil society groups plotting to overthrow an elected government. Thus, while one can reflect on Turkey's experience with modernity in the twentieth century as a glass half full, we must also reflect on its deficiencies and failures and try to fix them. Turkey's achievements clearly stemmed from multiparty, pluralist democracy, which still brings hope that the problems Turkey now faces can be solved with electoral participation and civil society mobilization.

PROCEDURAL FAIRNESS AND THE HEALING POWER OF PLURALIST DEMOCRACY

Turkey's twentieth century was about undoing a centuries-old cosmopolitan empire and creating a nation-state from this imperial legacy. During the traumatic developments of 1912–1924, some key ingredients of this diverse empire were excluded from the modernity project. The Turkish Republic tried to create a monolithic modern nation by molding the minds of its citizens and introducing a cultural revolution based on pro-Western secularism. This created a new set of problems and challenges because the Muslim majority population in Turkey in 1923 was also extremely diverse in ethnic, intellectual, and cultural orientation and naturally objected to a state attempting to shape the population into something else. Turkish elites feared losing sovereign control and exaggerated some of the threats, such as Kurdish separatism or religious reactions to secularism, for their own self-interest. Early on, elites argued that if a diverse Turkish population had full freedom it would lead to decentralization, fragmentation, or secession, and therefore they tried to tame, control, or even eliminate diversity in Turkish society.

It has been more than 90 years since the beginning of the Turkish Republic, and the state committed many injustices toward its citizens during this period in the name of ideologically rigid nationalism or Cold War political divisions. Yet, despite all the dark sides of this history, Turkey managed to keep a united nation not just by coercion but also by persuasion. In that process, a functioning pluralist democracy since 1950, despite multiple interruptions by cyclical military coups, contributed most to the formation of relative stability and allowed a learning process in which citizens accepted each other's differences. Turkish democracy evolved while passing through a twisted road with ups and downs, with violent episodes and oppressive cycles, including events such as the execution of a former prime minister (Adnan Menderes) on made-up charges in the aftermath of the 1960 coup, the bombing of Alevi Kurdish villages by the Turkish air force in late 1930s, and the bombing of the Turkish parliament by coup plotters as recently as July 2016. Gradually, however, the state was forced to acknowledge those incidents and today, many past experiences with victimization are debated freely in public, occasionally resulting in official apologies.

This recognition of past mistakes is not complete, and there is no guarantee that similar wrongdoing by the Turkish state or by any of the existing political movements will not occur in the future. Moreover, democracy has its own shortcomings as it is vulnerable to processes of polarization and the restriction of minority rights due to majoritarian hegemony. But it was pluralist democracy that sheltered the Turkish Republic from internal collapse and civil wars.[10] The internalization of the culture of democracy also prompted mass public protests against the coup attempt of July 2016 that helped defeat the military intervention.

The resilience of the multiparty democracy experiment in Turkey since 1950 gave Turkish citizens hope that they could organize to articulate their frustrations and demands and eventually end discrimination and suffering. In the first 27 years of the Turkish Republic, the political system amounted to one-party authoritarian rule, but from the beginning of multiparty electoral politics in 1950 to today, all Turkish elections have been free and fair, allowing a great degree of popular participation and expression of diversity. Even when the Turkish military intervened in democratic politics several times, the military immediately promised a return to civilian democratic politics. In short, a geopolitical commitment to the normative principles of democracy allowed Turkey to recover from its worst decades and find a mechanism for self-correction and improvement.

The success of Turkish democracy was partly due to the fact that Turkey has been a member of the NATO alliance and Turkish elites made membership into European Union a priority in their grand strategy. Thus, there were outside friends and allies that encouraged a return to democracy, even though those same friends, the United States especially, were the ones that supported various military coups, violating democratic governance in 1960 and in 1980. Yet the narrative of belonging to a democratic Western bloc of nations allowed pro-democracy forces in Turkey to mobilize and put pressure on antidemocratic elements. This experience may be compared to Greek politics in the sense that Greek democracy also triumphed against military intervention because of the EU vision. More important, comparing Turkey to Egypt illustrates the importance of commitment to the rules and principles of pluralist democracy and the positive role of the international and regional alliances and organizations in ensuring that democracy is respected and restored within a nation-state. Thus, Turkey was saved from an authoritarian regime similar to Italian and Spanish fascism and, after the death of Atatürk in 1938, did not deteriorate into a form of presidency for life or family dictatorship that existed in Bashar al-Assad's Syria, Hosni Mubarak's Egypt, and Hussein's Iraq. Thus, irrespective of all the imperfections and periodic suspension of multiparty democratic rule in Turkey, democracy triumphed. Today, many of the fierce opponents of the current government and President Recep Tayyip Erdoğan hope to change the country with democratic elections or legal, peaceful protests and not with military coups, violent methods, or foreign intervention. This explains why all of the opposition parties supported the elected government in defending democracy and resisting the July 2016 coup attempt by members of a religious movement identified with Muslim cleric Fethullah Gülen.

Thus, the most important lesson from the twentieth-century Turkish experience is the long-term healing power of a functioning pluralist democracy, despite its flaws and shortcomings, for a peaceful and prosperous world order. Turkey's success in establishing a functioning democracy after a history of militant secularism and military authoritarianism could be a model for Pakistanis and Egyptians seeking an end to the recurrence of military rule, extremism, and violence. It is also the hope of the opposition parties and political groups that challenge the concentration and misuse of power by elected governments.

GEOPOLITICS AS BOTH A BLESSING AND A CURSE

Although Turkish citizens benefited from the geopolitical alliance with NATO, the European Union, and the United States in ensuring the continuity of pluralist democracy, broader geopolitical conditions in the Middle East and Eurasia had a negative impact on the modern Turkish experience. Even when Turkish citizens were immune from devastating wars since 1923, they were naturally concerned about the shattered lives and suffering of millions of people in the broader Islamicate societies and the Middle East region in the second half of the twentieth century. Due to weak global governance institutions, great power interventions, and regional rivalries, the Middle East and North Africa region today has become a scene of failed states, sectarian conflicts, and unhealed wounds of multiple nations or minorities asking for their rights and dignity. Both the Eurocentric imperial order before the 1950s and the post–World War II American hegemonic order perpetuated rather than solved problems of rights violations, destabilization, and political conflicts in the Middle East. There is now a sense of pessimism about the current conditions and near future of the Middle East and North Africa region. The Turkish experience of the twentieth century was always closely linked to broader geopolitical rivalries and conditions.

Turkey's Ottoman predecessor in the first two decades of the twentieth century belonged to the club of European empires, even though Turkey was called the sick man of Europe. Ottoman Turkey was an empire, and it had an interest in prolonging and preserving the early twentieth-century imperial world order. Yet, due to the Muslim identity of the Ottoman dynasty, it was treated unequally by other empires. This exclusion coincided with admiration of Muslims living under British, Russian, French, and Dutch empires, and these colonized Muslims formed a connection with the Ottoman Sultan. The Ottoman Sultan, as Caliph, began to be seen as the voice and representative of racially alienated Muslim subjects of European empires in Asia and Africa. Just as the Japanese Empire's success proved that the yellow race is not inferior and Asians could be modern, the success of the Ottoman reforms, proved by its constitution and railways, was evidence for colonized Muslims that Islam and modernity can be compatible. Thus, the unique borderland position of the Ottoman Empire allowed its Muslim leaders to see and act on the imperial world order both from the center and from the periphery, and to try to reconcile the pro-imperial and anticolonial narratives. In fact, since early in the twentieth century, the Ottoman Muslim elites have struggled to reconcile the Eurocentric imperial narrative with the globalized Muslim narrative. Throughout the twentieth century, Turkish elites and the public kept this ambivalent position with regard to the international order, realistically trying to be a member of a defective international system while also aware of the problems and injustices of the world order from predominantly subaltern Muslim perspectives.

Throughout the nineteenth century, the Ottoman Empire prioritized its strategy as a civilized empire in alliance with other empires, especially the British Empire, trying to preserve the sovereignty of its cosmopolitan domains. The Ottoman elites argued that their empire should be part of the European imperial family and rule over Greeks and Armenians but still have prestige and respect among the Muslim subjects of European empires. Once the Ottoman Empire decided to join World War I on the side of Germany, however, the Ottoman elites strategically exploited the "Muslim world versus the Christian West" narrative in their propaganda, asking Indian Muslims, for example, to rebel against the British Empire. These calls for Muslim revolt against the British, Russian, Dutch, and French empires were highly irresponsible because the pan-Islamism of Indian Muslims was about gaining dignity and equality within various European empires, not rebelling against them. In some ways, the Ottoman propaganda during World War I abused the pan-Islamic view of imperial world order by trying to encourage Muslim rebellion against European empires.

A highly complex political narrative was constructed during the transition from the Ottoman Empire to the Turkish nation-state in the mid-1920s, when the Republic of Turkey was established after the military victories of Turkish nationalists against invading Greek armies. Turkish nationalism was redemptive in the sense that it is based on the story of salvation of the "victimized" Muslim majority populations of the declining Ottoman Empire. It may seem very paradoxical that the Muslim elites of the Ottoman Empire would, within a decade (1911–1923), move from being protectors of a multiethnic empire to anti-imperialist nationalism, with a strong historical consciousness of oppression and discrimination by the white Christian Western great powers.

After the establishment of the Turkish Republic in 1923, the founding fathers strategically based Turkey's vision of national sovereignty, dignity, and progress on an idealized and abstract narrative of European civilization spreading to non-European areas. When Turkish leaders used the idealized vision of secular and modern Europe as their role models, Europe was in interwar era turmoil, divided between ideologies and challenged by anticolonial nationalism. Europe as the normative home of modernity and enlightenment was still around as an intellectual project, even though the reality of Europe included the destructiveness of wars, racism, fascism, and genocide, and Turkish leaders were very aware of the discrepancies between those realities and the ideal. Yet, for their own strategic domestic reform agenda, they chose to embrace a vision of a normative Europe that would be more evident in the post-1990s European Union. It was during the westernization campaign that the Turkish Republic also faced a new question of Islam and secularism, which was not a political issue before the 1920s.

The pro-Western orientation of the Turkish Republic signified a conscious attempt to "leave the Muslim world." This can be compared to Japan's attempt to "leave Asia" (datsu-A) in the early Meiji period or after World War II. This geopolitical decision also required a difficult reorientation of the main narrative of the twentieth century from one of cosmopolitan imperialism to a Wilsonian narrative of national self-determination and pro-European cultural reform. Upon Ottoman Turkey's defeat in World War I, the Turkish war of independence and the establishment of the Turkish Republic continued to inspire many anticolonial Muslim nationalist organizations and movements. In the mid-1920s and afterward, the Turkish Republic refashioned a narrative of a universal world civilization centered in Europe and was determined to make Turkey a part of this Eurocentric political and cultural order. In that context, the Turkish parliament abolished the Caliphate and sent the last Caliph in Istanbul into exile in 1924. Turkey's long-term vision of the world assumed that other Muslim societies would also gradually gain their independence and form their own nation-states.

When the post–Ottoman era Turkish Republic abandoned earlier pan-Islamic identity narratives in favor of a new story of nationalist redemption, self-determination, westernization, and modernization, it became very successful in changing the perception of Turkey in European public opinion. With this new identity as a westernized secular society, not a Muslim one, the Turkish government's sovereignty was further assured, especially with praise in European and American media for the reform of women's status in Turkey. The Turkish Republic did indeed attain a higher level of legitimacy and stability due to converging narratives between Turkey and Europe. In this context, a secular (though nationalist) set of reformist values within Turkey gained the endorsement of Muslim elites across different post-colonial independent nations as a global Eurocentric narrative centered on the westernization of the Muslim world took hold. Yet the pan-Islamic narrative still persisted throughout the process of anticolonial struggles in Muslim societies, and portions of Muslim publics interpreted Turkish westernization as a betrayal of Muslim values and identity. People in different postcolonial Muslim majority countries have witnessed ongoing wars involving Muslims throughout the twentieth century, and eventually these wars became part of a narrative of the victimized Muslim world versus the colonial West. Especially after the Arab defeat in the 1967 Six Day War and the Soviet invasion of Afghanistan in 1979, older colonial-era narratives of the Muslim world versus the Christian West were refashioned for broader audiences by political groups such as Islamists. Samuel Huntington's clash of civilization thesis in the 1990s, written just after the genocide of Bosnian Muslims, was rearticulating a realist American view of this Muslim narrative. Pan-Islamic and later radical Islamist narratives reject the redemptive story of nationalism regaining Muslim dignity in a time of decolonization, and instead insist on a story of persistent humiliation of Muslim identity and "the Muslim world."

In the aftermath of World War II, Turkey's modernization narrative was refashioned by both the U.S. and Soviet camps, and in this context the earlier Turkish narrative of successful westernization of a Muslim society became highly useful for American attempts to promote its values to newly independent Muslim countries. Thus, U.S. modernization theory depicted Turkey as an ideal case of reform, development, democracy, and progress throughout the 1950s and the 1960s.[11] For anticolonial Muslim nationalists, Turkey was a good example of a Muslim society that freed itself from the humiliation of Western hegemony and gained dignity as an independent nation.

As various events—from the Arab-Israeli wars to the Soviet invasion of Afghanistan—subsequently led to pan-Islamic internationalism and new narratives of Muslim victimhood in the postcolonial, Cold War era, Turkish governments could no longer ignore developments in the Middle East. There were some Turkish leaders who almost wished they had built a wall between Turkey and the Middle East and made Turkey just a European country.[12] But historical, emotional, cultural, and identity links between Turkey and the other Muslim societies persisted. For example, the Turkish government could not be indifferent to the struggles of Algerians and secretly sent weapons to them, even when Turkey was an ally of France at NATO and once voted in favor of France on the issue of Algeria at a United Nations General Assembly meeting.

Due to the pressures of democratic politics, Turkish political elites had to balance the demands and implications of various narratives as much as they could. For example, Turkey voted against the partition of Palestine at the United Nations and increased its support to the Palestine Liberation Organization, while keeping full diplomatic and economic relations with Israel. To reconcile conflicting views of Arab-Israeli conflict, Turkey tried to contribute to the peace process between Israel and Palestine, thus turning its dilemmas into a negotiator's advantage. Similarly, the Turkish government gave as much diplomatic, military, and economic support as possible for the struggle of Bosnian Muslims when Yugoslavia disintegrated, because a genocide against Muslims in Europe was challenging Turkey's vision of becoming a Muslim majority member of the European Union. In the post–September 11 context, the Turkish government tried to dispel the clash of civilizations argument by initiating an Alliance of Civilization project at the UN level, hoping to show that competing narratives of the global order can actually be harmonious if Muslims and Europeans had a chance to understand each other and avoid making biased statements about essentialism repeated by radical groups. In fact, Turkey was shown as a model to disprove the radical and anti-Western Islamist narrative of the international system; instead, Turkey proved that a Muslim majority nation ruled by pious politicians could be a potential member of the European Union and a U.S. ally while defending the dignity and interests of oppressed Muslims such as Palestinians, Syrians, and Bosnians. In 2004, European leaders became tired of receiving phone calls from American presidents urging them to accept Turkey into the European Union. For the U.S. superpower, a European Turkey would prove that the war against terror is not a war against the Muslim world, and it would illustrate this point better than theoretical arguments.

The mission that Turkey assumed, as a harmonizer of dominant Eurocentric and Muslim narratives of the twentieth century, was a challenging task requiring immense intellectual and political skills. If the Turkish government does not openly defend the interests of the oppressed Muslim populations, it would be seen as a formerly great Muslim power that left "the Muslim world," and it would not have much influence over Muslim publics. If Turkey goes too far in critiquing and rejecting European and American policies in the Islamicate societies, it would be seen as too anti-Western. In many ways, reconciling the twentieth-century narrative of Europe and the Muslim world was a "mission impossible" for a fragile democracy like Turkey. With the complete collapse of the postcolonial state system in the Middle East and the rise of unimaginably nihilistic terrorist groups like ISIL (Islamic State of Iraq and the Levant), there is now confusion about what ideologies to use to effectively defeat the appeal of Muslim fundamentalism. It seems the Turkish government is still struggling to harmonize at least two moderate narratives of the global order: Muslim modernism and postcolonial Europeanism. But Turkey cannot succeed in this task alone because the international order itself is defective in tackling major issues such as human rights abuses, colonialism, ethnic hatred, sectarianism, and democratic governance. More important, the fallout from Turkey's support for the armed opposition to Syria's Assad regime since the summer of 2011 caused all of these narratives to implode, showing their illusionary and even delusionary character. The crisis of democracy and governance in Turkey is now even more difficult to tackle.

In conclusion, the current ambivalence about the Turkish experience with twentieth-century modernity may confirm the significance of this book, in the sense that this book tries to address the problems caused by scholarly and nonscholarly confusion about creating a global narrative about the meaning of twentieth-century world history. The Turkish case study contains all the positive and negative traits and characteristics of the twentieth-century world history experience, including the inability to reach agreement on a coherent and consistent narrative about this century. But Turkish democracy also needs the moral clarity and guidance of a new synthetic global vision for embracing the achievements of the twenty-first century and overcoming its failures, so it can then move forward and create a better life for its citizens as well as a peaceful regional order. Turkish democracy needs the delicate support of its allies— from Europe and from the United States, India, and Japan—to recover from its failures and bolster its foundation. Turkey's successful journey to political modernity is essential for the creation of an international world order in both West Asia and beyond.

NOTES

1. Zygmunt Bauman, *Modernity and the Holocaust* (Ithaca, NY: Cornell University Press, 1989.)

2. For works on the dark side of twentieth-century modernity in the German experience, see Detlev Peukert, *Weimar Republic: The Crisis of Classical Modernity*, trans. Richard Deveson (New York: Hill and Wang, 1989); Detlev Peukert, *Inside Nazi Germany: Conformity, Opposition, and Racism in Everyday Life*, trans. Richard Deveson (New Haven, CT: Yale University Press, 1987); Michel Foucault, *Discipline and Punish: The Birth of the Prison* (New York: Pantheon, 1977); and J. F. Lyotard, *The Postmodern Condition: A Report on Knowledge* (Minneapolis: University of Minnesota Press, 1984).

3. Jurgen Habermas, *The Philosophical Discourse of Modernity*, trans. Frederick G. Lawrence (Cambridge, MA: MIT Press, 1987). See also Richard Bernstein, *Habermas and Modernity* (Cambridge, MA: MIT Press, 1985).

4. Harry Harootunian, *Overcome by Modernity: History, Culture, and Community in Interwar Japan* (Princeton, NJ: Princeton University Press, 2000); Timothy Snyder, *Bloodlands: Europe between Hitler and Stalin* (New York: Basic Books, 2010).

5. Samuel Moyn, *The Last Utopia: Human Rights in History* (Cambridge, MA: Belknap Press of Harvard University Press, 2010).

6. Roger R. Trask, *The United States Response to Turkish Nationalism and Reform, 1914– 1939* (Minneapolis: University of Minnesota Press, 1971).

7. Walter Cronkite, "The Incredible Turk," CBS Documentary, produced by Burton Benjamin, 1958, available at https://www.youtube.com/watch?v =BjySoi2PRow.

8. Walter Weiker, *The Modernization of Turkey: From Ataturk to the Present Day* (New York: Holmes & Meier, 1981); Sibel Bozdogan and Resat Kasaba, *Rethinking Modernity and National Identity in Turkey* (Seattle: University of Washington Press, 1997).

9. Mehmet Dosemeci, *Debating Turkish Modernity: Civilization, Nationalism, and the EEC* (New York: Cambridge University Press, 2013).

10. Nilufer Göle, *The Forbidden Modern: Civilization and Veiling* (Ann Arbor: University of Michigan Press, 1996). Göle's book, which highlights the discontent of

Turkish modernization and secularism, can be contrasted with three other books that celebrated its achievements: Niyazi Berkes, *The Development of Secularism in Turkey* (New York: Routledge, 1998); Bernard Lewis, *The Emergence of Modern Turkey* (Oxford: Oxford University Press, 1968); and Daniel Lerner, *The Passing of Traditional Society: Modernizing the Middle East* (Glencoe, IL: Free Press, 1958).

11. Suhnaz Yilmaz, "Challenging the Stereotypes: Turkish-American Relations in the Inter-war Era," *Middle Eastern Studies* 42, no. 2 (March 2006): 223–237; Roger R. Trask, "The 'Terrible Turk' and Turkish-American Relations in the Interwar Period," *Historian* 33, no. 1 (November 1970): 40–53; John M. VanderLippe, "Racism and the Making of American Foreign Policy: The 'Terrible Turk' as Icon and Metaphor," *Research in Politics and Society* 6 (1999): 47–63.

12. Ahmet Serdar Akturk, "Arabs in Kemalist Turkish Historiography," *Middle Eastern Studies* 46, no. 5 (2010): 633–653.

5. CHINA'S "PROLONGED RISE": A TWENTIETH-CENTURY TALE AND ITS TWENTY-FIRST-CENTURY IMPLICATIONS

Chen Jian

One of the greatest tales of the twentieth century, as viewed from an early twenty-first-century vantage point, is the decline and resurgence of China as a great power on the world scene. Emerging from this tale is the large phenomenon now widely known as "China's rise." Indeed, entering the twenty-first century, the extraordinary magnitude and profound meanings of China's rise have been more visible than ever before, presenting the whole world a prospect mixing enormous opportunities with huge challenges now and in the decades to come. How to deal with them, by catching the opportunities and managing the challenges, becomes a question of utmost importance for world peace and prosperity that requires qualified and insightful answers. Given that China is the country with the largest population, second-largest economy, and third-largest territorial size in the world, the importance of this issue is self-evident.

There are different ways to answer the question, to be sure. In this chapter, I adopt a historical approach by putting China's rise—or, as I will discuss, its "prolonged rise"—into the larger context of its twentieth-century experience characterized by crises, wars, revolutions, and finally, unprecedented reforms. While doing so, I try to explain, from a Chinese perspective, what driving forces and dynamics generated China's rise, why it has to be looked on as a complicated and prolonged process, and what opportunities and challenges it presents to the twenty-first-century world, and how they might be dealt with.

RISE OF CHINESE NATIONALISM

Until the mid-nineteenth century, China—reigned then by the Manchu-Qing dynasty—was the world's largest economy. Yet, beginning with the Qing's defeat in the 1839–1842 Sino-British Opium War, China quickly fell into a series of deep domestic and international crises, which the Qing government was unable to cope with. In China's external relations, the Central Kingdom's "tribute system" was collapsing, replaced by a treaty system, one that was dominated by Western imperialist countries and alien to China's own age-old patterns of handling relations with other parts of the world.

Toward the end of the century, China already sank into a series of seemingly insurmountable crises. In the 1894–1895 Sino-Japanese War, the Qing was miserably defeated and signed the Treaty of Shimonoseki, in which China lost Taiwan and had to pay a huge amount of indemnity to Japan. Three years later, the 1898 Reform, with the goal of transforming China's economy and education and changing its weak-country status, failed. Around the same time, Western powers and Japan were planning and acting to claim "spheres of influence" in various parts of China. The very survival of "China" was seriously at stake.

In the first summer of the twentieth century, in response to the Boxer Rebellion, an international coalition composed of eight powers invaded China and occupied Beijing. The Qing court then signed the Boxer Protocol with them. In addition to having to pay an even larger indemnity, China lost control of its own custom tariff collection rights. The country was in a shambles.

The Qing government had no choice but, as a last resort, began a series of reforms, allegedly for the purpose of eventually changing China into a constitutional monarchy, to cope with the crisis situation. But it came too little and too late. In 1911, an anti-Qing uprising quickly turned into a nationwide revolution that overthrew the Manchu-Qing Empire and established the Republic of China.

It soon turned out that although the Chinese Revolution of 1911 succeeded in destroying a dynasty, it failed to create a genuine republic. Following the collapse of a strong central authority, warlordism emerged to politically divide China, as well as to undermine the Chinese people's hope of their country emerging as a respected power in the world. China's crises deepened.

All of this nurtured the rise of modern Chinese nationalism. Underlying it was the powerful Chinese victim mentality, and it was unique in that the Chinese belief in China being a victimized member of the modern international community formed such a sharp contrast with the age-old Central Kingdom concept (which regarded China as the civilization in toto). Accompanying this was the emergence of the intellectual and cultural upheaval known as the "New Culture Movement," in which many radical Chinese intellectuals criticized the deficiencies of China's "old culture" in sharp or even iconoclastic ways. The door to more radical revolutions was open wider.

In 1914, the Great War broke out. With the hope of reclaiming the "rights, interests, and privileges" lost in modern times, China joined the Entente powers and entered the war, a move that, as it so turned out, placed China on history's right side. In postwar peacemaking, the Chinese viewed U.S. President Woodrow Wilson's introduction of his "Fourteen Points" as bright light shining over the earth in an otherwise dark sky. In particular, they were inspired by Wilson's notions of abolition of secret diplomacy, national self-determination, democracy, and guarantees of independence and territorial integrity of weaker countries. Chen Duxiu, a Peking University professor who would later become a main founder of the Chinese Communist Party (CCP), even called Wilson "the first good man under heaven."[1]

But the actual development of the Paris Peace Conference made the Chinese deeply disappointed. In May 1919, when the Paris Conference imposed on China the deal of allowing Japan to take over the prewar German sphere of influence in China's Shandong Peninsula, President Wilson yielded to other powers at the last minute. The long-accumulated nationalist sentiment among the intellectuals and, especially, young students burst into a series of high-profile mass protests. Thus came into being the May Fourth Movement.

This was the time that the Bolshevik-led Russian Revolution was increasingly gaining influence among the Chinese, and radical Chinese intellectuals in particular. What made the Russian Revolution attractive to them was its anti-imperialist rhetoric and promises of bringing about universal justice and equality on earth. In 1921, the Chinese Communist Party was established. In the early and mid-1920s, with Moscow's backing, the Chinese Nationalist and Communist parties formed a "united front" to wage an anti-imperialist "Great Revolution."

This revolutionary episode, however, was short-lived. In 1927, the Nationalist Party leader Jiang Jieshi successfully waged a bloody anti-Communist coup. The next year, when Jiang established the Nationalist government in Nanjing, he meant to bring about another transformative revolution in China following his visions of modernity and ambitious plans to modernize China. Thus began what in Chinese history was known as the "Nanjing decade." From the outset, Jiang was facing serious domestic challenges, from the warlords who continuously challenged his authority and leadership role and, especially, from the CCP rebels (such as Mao Zedong), who carried out guerrilla wars in the countryside. But it was Japan's aggression against China that finally made Jiang's state-building and modernization drive during the Nanjing decade fruitless.

In the years between the two world wars, no development in China and East Asia had produced more detrimental effects than Japan's choice of identifying itself as one of the "have-nots," rather than one of the "haves." Beginning with the Manchurian Incident of September 1931, Japan carried out continuous actions of aggression against China, first in Manchuria and then in Northern China. Facing the Japanese threat, Jiang risked losing his status as China's national leader to focus on suppressing the communist rebels. By the mid-1930s, it seemed that Jiang was only inches away from finally eliminating the communist rebellion. Then, in December 1936, two of Jiang's generals—who opposed his policy of "putting suppression of the CCP ahead of resistance against Japan"—kidnapped him in Xi'an. Jiang was forced to accept the condition of stopping the civil war against the CCP so that the whole nation would unite to cope with Japan's threat. The next year, the Sino-Japanese War broke out.

Japan's invasion of China was from the beginning an integral part of its quest for Asia-Pacific hegemony. By joining Berlin and Rome in the Tripartite Pact, Tokyo also made a fatal mistake in making itself the enemy of the Allies. China, with its persistence in its war against Japan, became a member of the Allies. Once again China stood on history's correct side whereas Japan stood on the wrong side.

All of this was by no means accidental. Even before the United States formally entered the war, in August 1941 President Franklin D. Roosevelt, together with Prime Minister Winston Churchill of the United Kingdom, issued the Atlantic Charter. It formed the normative foundation of the Allies, and its letters and spirit were profoundly interconnected with the Wilsonian perceptions and designs of a new world order, extending the "Wilsonian moment" to the dawn of a new age, which China embraced wholeheartedly. In comparison, everything Japan had done leading up to the Pacific War, a practice belonging to the fading-away era of imperialism and colonialism, was against the coming of such an age.

During the war years, the political and military balance of power within China changed. The CCP gained a heaven-sent chance of survival and development. Holding high the banner of nationalism (and then also the banner of democracy, defined in the CCP's own way), the CCP greatly expanded its strength and influence. In contrast, Jiang's government, burdened by widespread corruption, runaway inflation, military incompetence, and an image of "political dictatorship," faced deepening crisis toward the later years of the war.

Largely because of the serious domestic challenges presented by the CCP, Jiang was unable to give attention to China's maritime rights issue from the standpoint of a strong power in the concluding phase of the war.

China's war of resistance against Japan ended in August 1945 when Japan surrendered unconditionally to the Allies. Peace, however, did not come to China's war-torn land. Almost immediately a civil war between the Nationalists and the Communists erupted in China. It quickly merged with the emerging Cold War. A "CCP-Moscow versus Nationalists-Washington" alignment came into being. Despite the Nationalists' initial superiority in military strength and control of resources and material support (though limited) from the United States, Jiang and his regime, suffering from political corruption, economic collapse, and military failure, lost the war to the Communists in three short years. In 1949, the People's Republic of China (PRC) was born.

THE "NEW CHINA"

The PRC—the "new China"—was from the outset a "revolutionary country." Mao Zedong announced to the whole world that "we, the Chinese, have stood up."[2] This was a huge legitimacy statement that, first and foremost, took the Chinese as its primary audience. Mao substantiated the statement by establishing two fundamental missions for his "revolution after revolution": to change China into a land of universal justice, equality, and prosperity; and, by challenging and destroying the "old" world, to revive China's central position in the international community. The PRC under Mao's reign constantly challenged the legitimacy of the existing international order, which Mao and his comrades believed to be the result of Western domination and thus inimical to revolutionary China.

Even before the PRC's establishment, Mao announced that the new China would "lean to one side," the side of the Soviet Union and the communist bloc.[3] In February 1950, Beijing signed a strategic alliance with Moscow. The treaty's presumed main enemy was not the United States, but Japanese militarists. In a sense, this was a revelation of Mao's and the CCP's intention to provide larger legitimacy to the Sino-Soviet alliance by appealing to the Chinese people's memory of Japan's history of aggression against China.

A more fundamental legitimacy-building effort on the part of Mao and the CCP was found in their adoption of an anti-Japanese-imperialism song, composed in the 1930s, "March Song of the Righteous Volunteers," as the PRC's national anthem.

In June 1950, the Korean War, the first major hot war during the Cold War, broke out. The United States was quickly involved. Four months later, Mao and the Beijing leadership decided to send "Chinese volunteers" to Korea. The Korean War changed into a major Chinese-American war.

Why did China enter the Korean War? This issue has been discussed and debated heatedly among concerned scholars. In my view, security and geopolitical concerns certainly played an important role. After all, Korea is China's neighbor and, in history, it once belonged to China's spheres of influence. For Beijing's leaders, allowing Korea to be controlled by hostile imperialist forces posed grave threats to China's security interests. On a deeper level, though, Mao and his comrades made the decision to enter the Korean War mainly to exploit the pressure created by the external crisis in ways that would enhance the CCP's control of China's state and society. China's intervention in Korea also represented a crucial step by Mao and his comrades to revive China's central position in East Asian international affairs, which in turn would serve as a powerful source of domestic mobilization. Mao hoped to use China's victory in Korea to prove to the world and, especially, to China's own people that indeed "the Chinese have stood up."[4]

U.S. policymakers and military planners (and General Douglas MacArthur in particular) did not believe that China, so backward and so weak, would enter the war. Mao knew this, and was genuinely offended. Compared with U.S. hostility toward China, what was more furious and enraging to the Chinese was the perceived American disdain of China and the Chinese as backward and, worse, inferior. Anti-American-imperialism became a main theme of extensive domestic mobilization throughout China in the Korean War years and long after.

The Cold War led to profound division between the Allies of the Second World War. In Asia, this was most evidently demonstrated by the difficulty involved in the making of the peace treaty with Japan. When China and the United States were engaged in the war in Korea, the San Francisco Conference for concluding peace with Japan was convened. The PRC did not attend it. Although China was one of the "Big Four" of the Allies during World War II, the treaty of peace with Japan signed at San Francisco was without any input from Beijing. From the beginning, Beijing challenged the San Francisco System as a seriously flawed peace settlement for East Asia that was a product of the Cold War.

There are deeper meanings, ones concerning the normative and moral foundation of a "just peace," behind Beijing's grievance. As China was a principal member of the victorious Allies during the Second World War, Beijing's leaders believed that any postwar peace settlement involving China's interests would not be legitimate if China was not involved in the settlement's making. The San Francisco System, therefore, did not have any bounding power on China. Rather, it obscured the normative and moral foundation of the existing international system and structure, building into them a potential cause for instability and crisis in the long run. It is here that one finds some of the deep sources of the territorial disputes China now is involved with in the East and South China Seas.

In the wake of the Korean War, the Sino-Soviet alliance was significantly enhanced and upgraded. Seeing China's great strategic value, Moscow's post-Stalin leadership provided China with vast and high-quality support in the remaining years of the 1950s that probably should be called the greatest transfer of modern industry from one country to another on a scale that the world had not seen before and, most likely, since. Consequently, China's industrialization or modernization drive was brought to a much higher level within a decade's time.

However, in the late 1950s, Mao and the Beijing leadership made the decision to split with Moscow. Why? Domestic considerations again were the main reason. China's "younger brother" status in its alliance with the Soviet Union was in fundamental conflict with the CCP's China-centered legitimacy narrative. Entering the 1960s, when Mao was pushing China toward the "Great Proletarian Cultural Revolution," as he announced, and preventing a "Soviet-style capitalist restoration" from happening in China, he contended that

"Soviet revisionists" and "social-imperialists" had long carried out a policy of "great power chauvinism" toward China, characterizing Moscow as a serious threat to Chinese sovereignty and independence. No other Chinese leader was in a position to rebut such Maoist rhetoric reinforced by revolutionary nationalism.

In the 1950s and 1960s, a total confrontation persisted between China and the United States. Policymakers in Washington believed that, compared with the Soviet Union, Communist China was a "more daring, therefore more dangerous enemy." Although the emphasis of America's global strategy lay in Europe and the Soviet Union was America's presumed primary enemy, a large portion of America's resources were being deployed in East Asia for coping with the "Chinese Communist threats" there. In 1954, when President Dwight Eisenhower formally introduced the "domino theory" in the context of growing communist power and influence in Indochina, he had in his mind the grave impact if the practice of the Chinese Revolution were allowed to spread unchecked in East Asia.[5] The two Taiwan Strait crises of 1954–1955 and 1958 brought the United States to the verge of another direct military confrontation with China. In managing these crises, military planners in Washington even considered the possibility of using nuclear weapons.[6] Largely because of worries of threats from Communist China, the United States entered the Vietnam War, the "longest war" in American history.

The keys here were misperceptions and misjudgment on the part of U.S. policymakers and military planners about China and its intentions. In spite of its aggressive international behavior, Mao's China was not an expansionist power as the term is typically defined in Western strategic discourse. While using force, largely because of domestic-centered and legitimacy-related concerns, what the Chinese leaders hoped to achieve was not the PRC's direct control of foreign territory or resources, but the spread of the Chinese Revolution's influence on "hearts and minds" around the world. It was aspiration for "centrality," rather than pursuit of "dominance," that characterized the external policy of Mao's China. This has important implications for understanding China's external behavior then, today, and in the future.

Indeed, as shown by a series of cases, Chinese foreign policy and security strategy during the Maoist era were defined by domestic needs and considerations, rather than by external goals—certainly not by goals of territorial expansionism.

The 1954–1955 Taiwan Strait crisis occurred at the same time that Mao and the CCP leadership were preparing for domestic mobilization associated with "socialist transformations" in China's countryside and cities. The Taiwan Strait crisis of 1958 erupted when Mao's Great Leap Forward was sweeping across China. China's involvement in the Vietnam War and Beijing's high-volume propaganda about the Chinese people's determination to support the Vietnamese people's war against the U.S. imperialists correlated with the making of the Great Proletarian Cultural Revolution. For Mao's "revolution after revolution" programs, a revolutionary foreign policy was always of great relevance. In fact, in the early years of the PRC, such a foreign policy helped make Mao's various state and societal transformation programs powerful *unifying* and *national* themes supplanting many local, regional, or factional concerns. When Mao's revolutions were losing the Chinese people's support, a foreign policy like this served as a useful and effective way through which Mao might maintain both his authority and the momentum of his revolutionary programs. Consequently, Mao and his colleagues seemed to have been unafraid of using force in dealing with foreign policy crises.

Yet China and United States avoided another direct military confrontation over Vietnam or elsewhere in East Asia. Both Chinese and U.S. leaders regarded the other as an enemy, but they were willing to count on the consistency and "limited rationality" of the other side. What was interesting was that there existed a specific yet critical form of "mutual confidence" in Beijing's and Washington's strategic thinking in the wake of the Korean War. Without yielding to the legitimacy of the other side's policy goals and ideological commitments, both sides nevertheless had developed a conviction of the other side's willingness and capacity to persist in a limited and pragmatic course of action in accordance with its own rationale, logic, and perceived interests. This "mutual confidence" was clearly demonstrated in Washington's and Beijing's "signaling" in 1965 and 1966 about what they might do and might not do toward the escalating war in Vietnam, which contributed to making the Vietnam War a "limited war" as the military conflicts went on.[7] Even in the heyday of Chinese-American confrontation, leaders of both countries demonstrated that they were rational actors.

In the late 1960s, when confrontation between Beijing and Washington seemed to have reached the worst point in two decades, the Chinese-American rapprochement occurred almost overnight. With President Richard Nixon's visit to Beijing in February 1972, both China and the world had been changed.

The Chinese-American rapprochement dramatically shifted the balance of power between the United States and the Soviet Union. By jointly perceiving the Soviet Union as a primary enemy, Beijing and Washington entered into a "tacit alliance," as described by Henry Kissinger.[8] More important, the rapprochement changed the essence of the Cold War. It also obscured the Cold War's basic feature as a contest between communism and liberal capitalism as two competing paths heading toward modernity. In the final analysis, Beijing's shifting sides to the capitalist West buried the shared consciousness among communists in the world that communism was a workable solution to the problems created by the worldwide process of modernization.

Beijing's new relations with Washington also changed the structure and orientation of East Asian international relations. As Washington failed to consult with Tokyo in advance about its changing policy toward Beijing, a "Nixon shock" rocked Japan immediately after the U.S. president's announcement of his plan to visit China. After all, the U.S.-Japanese security alliance was always Washington-centered. Japan soon followed suit. Only months after Nixon's historic China visit, Beijing and Tokyo established diplomatic relations. It was the willingness on the part of both that made the process of China-Japan normalization smooth. Mao and the Beijing leadership had long decided that, as a gesture of Chinese moral superiority and friendship to the Japanese people, they would not pursue war reparations from Japan. In meetings between

Chinese premier Zhou Enlai and Japanese prime minister Kakuei Tanaka, the two leaders came up with a de facto understanding to shelve the two countries' differences in sovereignty claims over the Diaoyu/Senkaku Islands so that "more urgent and important matters, such as establishment of diplomatic relations, could be resolved without delays."[9] By doing so, Beijing avoided a direct challenge to the San Francisco System, so as not to cause difficulty for the new U.S.-China relationship.

China's rapprochement with the United States created new space for changes in China's development policies. In 1972–1973, Beijing approved 26 major projects on importing whole-set equipment and technologies from Western countries and Japan, with a total budget of US$4.3 billion.[10] Implementation of these projects would represent a first major step toward bringing China into the "world market" dominated by Western capitalist countries.

From a Chinese perspective, in many key senses the Cold War did not end in the early 1990s but rather in the 1970s, along with the Chinese-American rapprochement. This is a crucial point for understanding not only why "communist" China survived the end of the Cold War but also why and how China's drive for modernity continued in the post–Cold War era.

ECONOMIC REFORM AND OPENING UP

Mao died on September 9, 1976. In less than two years, Deng Xiaoping emerged as China's paramount leader, launching a reform and opening-up project aimed at modernizing China while simultaneously coping with the profound legitimacy crisis that Mao had bequeathed to post-Mao China. The specific ways in which Deng and the CCP leadership envisioned and carried out the project, while easing some of the old legitimacy pressure, created new legitimacy challenges for the Chinese state and doomed the international communist movement.

The "tacit alliance" between China and the United States developed continuously under Deng. In the meantime, there were also important changes in Deng's perception of Chinese-American relations. Throughout the Maoist era, markets and the pursuit of profits were treated as values and practices inimical to genuine socialism. By introducing reform and opening up policies, Deng began to perceive China's path toward modernity in a very different light. Reportedly, when Deng was on his way to visit the United States in January 1979, he said that all of those developing countries on the side of the United States had been successful in their modernization drive, whereas all of those against the United States had not been successful. He said that China should be on the side of the United States.[11] China thus was changing from an "outsider" into an "insider" of the existing international order.

Against this background, China and Japan signed a treaty of peace and cooperation in 1978. Japan began to provide China with a huge amount of "development loans" with no or very low interest. Implicitly, at least from a Chinese perspective, this was also a remedy for war reparations from Japan that China had waived. Deng Xiaoping conferred with Japanese leaders and announced to the public that the differences between China and Japan over Diaoyu/Senkaku would be continuously shelved.[12]

Deng's reform and opening policies, however, were highly unbalanced in essence: emphasis was placed on developing the Chinese economy, leaving politics a forbidden zone. And this uneven process of development finally brought China's state and society to the verge of a serious crisis in 1989. When Beijing's students and citizens held protests and occupied Tiananmen Square to demand a "more comprehensive reform project," Deng and other party elders ordered troops to crack down, ending the protest in bloodshed on June 4, 1989.

The Tiananmen tragedy stunned the entire world. In a sense, it also triggered a chain of historic events that made 1989 a landmark year in world history. Two years later, the Soviet Union and the Soviet bloc in Eastern Europe collapsed. In turn, the global Cold War came to an end.

The Chinese Communist state survived the tremendous shockwaves of the end of the Cold War. In retrospect, this was largely because long before the late 1980s China had withdrawn from the global Cold War and become deeply involved in the process of "reform and opening to the outside world." Reform—and in particular the substantial economic growth that it generated and the continuous improvement of China's international status—enhanced the image among the Chinese people that indeed "we the Chinese have stood up," thus creating the space for Deng and the CCP leadership to deal with the accumulated legitimacy challenge facing the Chinese state.

Deng ordered the Tiananmen crackdown. But he also understood that only by pushing forward the reform and opening process would the Chinese Communist state be able to deal with the profound legitimacy challenge it was facing. In early 1992, Deng, at age 88, made a series of statements during a tour to southern China, emphasizing that reforms should be carried out in deeper ways. The CCP leadership then formally adopted a "socialist market economy" as the goal of China's regenerated reform and opening project. What followed was China's rapid economic growth that has lasted for over two decades.

CHINA TODAY

More than 20 years have passed since the end of the Cold War, and China is now at the crossroads. China's economic growth is extraordinary and real—in 2010, China surpassed Japan to become the second-largest economy in the world. The Maoist political cruelty is long gone with no hope of returning. Chinese society has become more diverse and plural. The Chinese economy has been further integrated into the world market and China also has played positive and constructive roles in many important aspects of world affairs (remember, for example, China's highly positive role in controlling the impact of the 2008 worldwide financial crisis), demonstrating its desire and capacity to be a responsible stakeholder—indeed, a genuine "insider"—in the increasingly integrated world community.

China today is not Wilhelm II's Germany in the First World War; it is not Hitler's Germany, Mussolini's Italy, or militarist Japan in the Second World War; and it is not the Soviet Union in the Cold War.

China's relations with the United States today are fundamentally different from Soviet-American relations during the Cold War. First, unlike the Soviet Union, China today does not present itself as an alternative—in terms of how the mainstream path toward modernity/postmodernity should and can be defined—to the American patterns of development and ways of life. Second, unlike the Soviet Union, China today is an integral part of the world economic system and institutions, not an "outsider." Third, unlike the Soviet Union, China today does not have its own military alliance or bloc that stands in confrontation with America's worldwide alliance system. The overwhelming majority of the problems between China and the United States have also existed between America and its Western allies in the recent past (including Japan, if we still remember the "America's coming war with Japan" rhetoric of the 1980s and early 1990s).

Yet China's rise has its own dilemmas and hurdles. Like the situation in the twentieth-century tale that I have told, the biggest challenges facing China are from within, not without. First and foremost among them is what has perplexed China throughout the complicated process of its "prolonged rise"—the legitimacy challenge.

In the past two decades, the Chinese "Communist" state has continuously taken full advantage of China's rapid economic growth, linking it with Mao's "we the Chinese have stood up" rhetoric and changing it into a key justification of the PRC's legitimacy narrative. However, the "legitimacy" so defined is no more than a "performance-based" one that counts on the belief that China's rapid economic growth may last forever.

Furthermore, China's phenomenal economic expansion has been accompanied by profound and continuous transformations of Chinese society, releasing new and powerful social forces the country has never seen in its long history. The convergence of a reduced economic growth rate and increasing social and political diversity will inevitably challenge the country's political structure. In the meantime, the legacy of China's age of revolutions has been reflected in the breakdown of the moral norms of Chinese society, a phenomenon that has deepened as a result of rampant materialism in the reform and opening-up era.

If China is to become a respected and great power in the world, it is essential for the Chinese to get out of the shadow of their victim mentality and the nationalist sentiment associated with it. But this is also a task that needs to be fulfilled with the cooperation of others. In this respect, Japan is in a position to play a salient role, especially as Japan had imposed wars of aggression against China in modern history, serving as a powerful source in the making and sustaining of the Chinese victim mentality. To sincerely accept and apologize for its war guilt will make Japan stronger and more respected in China, East Asia, and throughout the world, which is also of critical importance for confirming Japan's own identity as a genuine "insider" of the existing international system and structure. As a first step to reduce tension between China and Japan, with the prospect of bringing relations between the two countries to a more normal status, the two countries should, as they did after establishing diplomatic relations, shelve their differences on sovereignty claims over the Diaoyu/Senkaku Islands.[13]

On a more basic level, China faces the challenge of how to envision and pursue political reforms aimed not only at maintaining and enhancing the functioning and capacity of the state but also introducing a structure characterized by power checking and balancing. The Chinese people also face the daunting task of building or rebuilding the moral foundation of society in their ongoing pursuit of modernity and postmodernity so that China's continuous rise will satisfy not only the people's improved material needs but also their search for the meaning of life. China still has a very long way to go in achieving these challenging goals.

NOTES

1. Chen Duxiu, *Duxiu wencun* [Chen Duxiu's Writings] (Hefei: Anhui renmin, 1987), 388.

2. Mao Zedong, "The Chinese People Have Stood Up," *Mao Zedong wenji* [A Collection of Mao Zedong's Writings] (Beijing: Renmin, 1995), 3:342–346.

3. Mao Zedong, "On the People's Democratic Dictatorship," *Mao Zedong xuanji* [Selected Works of Mao Zedong] (Beijing: Renmin, 1965), 4:1477.

4. For more substantial discussion on the subject, see Chen Jian, *China's Road to the Korean War: The Making of the Sino-American Confrontation* (New York: Columbia University Press, 1994).

5. *Public Papers of the Presidents: Dwight D. Eisenhower, 1954* (Washington, DC: Government Printing Office, 1960), 381–390.

6. For a good account of this issues, see H. W. Brands, "Testing Massive Retaliation: Credibility and Crisis Management in the Taiwan Strait," *International Security* 12, no. 4 (Spring 1988): 124–151. See also Gordon H. Chang, *Friends of Enemies: The United States, China, and the Soviet Union, 1948–1972* (Stanford, CA: Stanford University Press, 1990), 126–128, 189–190.

7. For a detailed examination of the Chinese-American "signaling" in 1965 over Vietnam, see James Hershberg and Chen Jian, "Informing the Enemy: Sino-American Signaling and the Vietnam War, 1965," in *Behind the Bamboo Curtain: China, Vietnam, and the World beyond Asia*, ed. Priscilla Roberts (Stanford, CA: Stanford University Press, 2006), 193–257.

8. Kissinger to Nixon, "My Trip to Peking, June 19–23, 1972," 6/27/72, Box 851, National Security Files, Nixon Presidential Material, National Archives, 2.

9. Zhang Xiangshan, "Recalling the Chinese-Japanese Negotiations on Restoring Diplomatic Relations," *Riben xukan* [Japan Studies] 1 (1998): 47. (Zhang was an adviser for Zhou Enlai.)

10. For reports on importing technology and whole-set equipment from the United States and other Western countries, see Li Xiaonian to Zhou Enlai et al., December 25, 1972, and January 4, 1972, *Jianguo yilai Li Xiaonian wengao* [Li Xiaonian's Manuscripts since the Formation of the PRC] (Beijing: Zhongyang wenxian, 2011), 3:189–190.

11. This information was gained from an August 2008 interview with a leading Chinese Communist Party historian and confirmed later through several other sources.

12. See, for example, Deng Xiaoping's conversation with Foreign Minister Sonoda Sunao of Japan, August 10, 1978, *Deng Xiaoping nianpu* [A Chronological Record of Deng Xiaoping] (Beijing: Zhongyang wenxian, 2004), 1:355.

13. In my view, the Diaoyu/Senkaku dispute is not about who should control the oil resources reportedly in existence in areas near the islands. It is not even about sovereignty claims over the islands, at least not as much as the general public has been led to believe. In the final analysis, it is about great power status, national pride, domestic representation and mobilization, and legitimacy and contemporary implications of the specific paths toward modernity and beyond. The dispute has served as a central test case in this respect for both countries in recent years.

6. THE TRANSFORMATION OF INDIA IN THE TWENTIETH CENTURY

Srinath Raghavan

Contemporary India is widely acknowledged to be a large and successful democracy, a fast-growing economy, and an aspirant and potential great power. It is accordingly tempting to tell the story of India's twentieth century in one of three ways: the establishment and consolidation of the world's most populous democracy; the long emergence of an economic powerhouse from a historically poor society; and the rise of India from a colony to a major power. These narratives would fit well with our current understandings of the key themes of global history in the twentieth century: the astonishing and unlikely success of liberal democracy as the most acceptable form of governance; the onset of a "golden age" of economic prosperity after the Second World War—a label that subsumes several processes such as globalization, urbanization, improvements in health, gender equality, and so forth; and the emergence of the United States as unprecedented hegemonic power in the international system along with other systemically important actors.

Yet each of these narratives about India's twentieth century would be decidedly partial. In the first place, they would suggest that these large trends were either self-contained or complete. What we need is an integrated account that underscores the interconnection between these processes as well as their open-ended character. For the transformations that India underwent in the twentieth century are neither complete nor wholly irreversible.

Further, we also need a narrative that shows the specificity of the Indian experience—and not just its commonalities with those of other countries. This is not to claim that India's trajectory in the twentieth century can be understood solely by recourse to internal structures and events—though much of Indian historiography operates in this insular mode. On the contrary, the global dimension is indispensable to making sense of India's journey through this period. Yet the fact remains that India's experience—especially in the second half of the twentieth century—was different in certain key respects. And this specificity should not be flattened out in the search for a global perspective. Indeed, these particularities may offer us more to think about when examining the challenges that we confront in the twenty-first century.

The story of India's twentieth century, I would suggest, is one of multiple, interconnected, nonlinear, and ongoing transformations: the consolidation of a modern state even as it transformed from a colonial state to a nation-state; the introduction and subsequent widening and deepening of democracy; the dilemmas of social reform in a deeply hierarchical culture; the many pathways of economic change in a society gripped by poverty; and the entry and consolidation of India as an important actor in the international system of states. The specificity of the Indian experience, particularly in the latter half of the past century, lies in the *simultaneity* of these processes.

Contemporary India's encounter with modernity—an omnibus term that bundles together such processes as the rise of a modern state and forms of governmentality, capitalist economic development, social individuation, secularization, nationalism, and democracy—differed sharply from that of the West, where various strands of change occurred at different points in time. Democracy, to take but one example, arrived in the West after the establishment of a capitalist economy and a secular state. At the same time, the Indian experience also differs from that of many non-Western or developing countries inasmuch as democracy remained a permanent feature on independent India's political landscape.

This chapter aims to paint this picture in broad brushstrokes. Although my treatment is thematic, it may be useful to note that these manifold changes across the twentieth century can be divided into four distinct historical periods: freedom and decolonization, from the end of the First World War to the end of the 1940s; postcolonial consolidation, from 1950 to the mid-1960s; the hinge years between the mid-1960s and the late 1980s (or the long 1970s); the era of reform and rise, from the early 1990s to the present. It may also be useful to bear in mind two salient structural features of the Indian experience. First, these transformations occurred against the backdrop of huge demographic change. India's population rose from 361 million in 1951 to 683 million in 1981 and 1,003 million in 2011. Second, they occurred in a society of bewildering diversity and multiple cleavages of language and ethnicity, religion and region, caste and class.

INDIA'S ENCOUNTER WITH MODERNITY

India's first brush with modernity took place through the colonial state. The British Empire in India began with a commercial bridgehead in Bengal in the mid-eighteenth century, but soon the East India Company acquired many trappings of contemporary European fiscal-military states. Over the next century and a half, the Company state expanded inexorably into other parts of India. Following the rebellion of 1857, the British Crown assumed direct control of the Indian empire. The Raj now began searching for conservative allies to buttress its rule and so strengthened the position of Indian princes and landlords. The need for indigenous collaborators and increased revenue also led to the expansion of the lower orders of the colonial bureaucracy, which was thrown open to educated Indians. In time, these classes would form the kernel of the nationalist movement that would challenge the colonial state's claims of benevolent rule over India.[1]

At the turn of the twentieth century, nationalist politics was very much an elitist affair. Formed in 1886, the Indian National Congress claimed to represent the Indian people, but in fact voiced the views of the educated Indian elites. Until the end of the First World War, nationalist politics was mostly "mendicant"—relying on petitions and supplication to get the colonial state to grant Indians greater political role and better economic prospects. Even the "extremist" wing of the Congress sought no more than "home rule," like Ireland, or dominion status, like Canada, Australia, and South Africa. It is worth recalling that even Mohandas K. Gandhi operated within this political framework and actively worked to recruit Indian soldiers to fight for the British Empire during the Great War.

The First World War had a transformative impact on Indian politics and announced the entry of India into the global twentieth century. Indian contribution to the war effort was significant. The Indian army expanded from a little over 100,000 men to 1.1 million—and some 60,000 of them never returned to their homes. Although India was a poor country, its economic contribution was also considerable. Despite attempts by the Ottoman Empire to fan the flames of jihad, Indian Muslims—including most soldiers— stood by the Raj. The Indians naturally hoped that their participation in the war effort would result in the grant of self-rule within the empire. But these hopes were brutally belied. The constitutional reforms in India announced at the end of the war were parsimonious: there was only a very limited extension of representative institutions. Indians were equally disappointed by U.S. President Woodrow Wilson's unwillingness to lean on the colonial powers to apply his principles to their empires.[2] Worse still was the use by the colonial state of wartime powers to crack down on public dissent—the most vicious instance being the massacre at Jallianwala Bagh in the Punjab.

It was against this backdrop that Gandhi stepped on to the center stage of nationalist politics. By deftly co-opting the movement among Indian Muslims against the abolition of the Ottoman Caliphate, Gandhi at once sought to build bridges between Hindus and Muslims and to widen the bases of nationalism far beyond the chambers of elite politicians. In successive waves of mobilization over the next three decades, Gandhi managed to draw into the nationalist movement large swathes of rural and urban India, although significant groups, especially the Muslims and the most downtrodden section of the Hindus—the so-called untouchables or depressed castes—were not substantially drawn to the Congress.

The colonial state responded by contesting Congress claims to represent all of India and by supporting the demands of groups such as Muslims and depressed castes. The onset of the Second World War deepened the Raj's propensity for divide and rule. The Indian National Congress made it clear that it would cooperate with the war effort only if an interim national government was formed immediately and India promised independence after the war. The outbreak of the massive "Quit India" revolt in the summer of 1942, led the British to put the Congress leaders behind bars for the remainder of the war. The Raj also gave a free run to the Muslim League, led by M. A. Jinnah, which had raised the demand for a separate "Pakistan" in March 1940.

The massive mobilization for war, however, convinced the British that they could not hold on to India by force. This time round, India provided no fewer than 2.5 million soldiers who fought in theaters stretching from Hong Kong to Italy. India's economic contribution was immense. By provisioning British and Allied forces, India emerged as one of the largest creditors to Britain. Wartime mobilization also imposed terrible privations on a poor country: some 3 million people perished in the famine in Bengal alone. The wartime churning of Indian society implied that the political stance adopted by the Raj after the Great War could not be replicated.[3]

Freedom however came with division. The massive ethnic violence and dislocation accompanying partition in mid-1947 placed an enormous strain on the postcolonial state in terms of curbing violence, succoring the victims, and planning for post-partition reconstruction. In this context, Jawaharlal Nehru and his Congress colleagues put on hold their plans for thoroughgoing reform of public institutions, especially the bureaucracy and police. The postcolonial state thus carried over the institutional characteristics of the colonial state, particularly its overbearing officialdom. If anything, the role of the state would expand dramatically during Nehru's years in office from 1947 to 1964. Nehru's plans for economic development (discussed later in this chapter) relied considerably on the bureaucracy. This was not just because he envisaged a large public sector in the economy, but also because his social democratic inclinations were at odds with the views of his own party.

THE INTRODUCTION OF DEMOCRACY

The notion of a "transfer of power" may have appealed to the vanity of the departing colonizers, but it does not capture the historical complexity of this period. While there were important continuities with the Raj, there were also decisive ruptures. The traditional aristocracy of India comprising the princes and landlords—groups that that had been bulwark of the Raj—was cut to size in almost one swoop. The princes were forced to integrate their territories with the Indian Union: their pretensions to sovereignty were rapidly punctured by the postcolonial state, if necessary by force. The landlords were similarly brought to heel by initiating land reforms. These reforms primarily benefited the upper strata of the peasantry, hitherto the managers rather than the owners of land. From the onset of the Great Depression, which led to the immiseration of the Indian peasantry, these groups had stood squarely behind the Congress party. Land reforms in independent India are usually criticized as insufficiently revolutionary for not transferring land to the tiller. This is true, but the removal of the landlords alongside the princes was a major step in its own right. We only have to compare the politics of India with those of Pakistan to realize its significance.

The most significant rupture with the Raj was the adoption in January 1950 of a republican constitution, which gave franchise to all adult Indians. The importance of this move is hard to overstate.[4] India had none of the background conditions—education, economic development, ethnic homogeneity—that political scientists deem essential for the success of democratic government. In 1951, 82 percent of India's population was illiterate. Over the past half-century India's economic growth had been dismal. And despite the creation of Pakistan, India remained a remarkably diverse country. Equally noteworthy was the grant of suffrage to women from the outset. Above all, it was sheer chutzpah to introduce of democratic politics in an extraordinarily unequal society. The Indian caste system, while by no means static or unchanging, was one of the most intricate and exclusionary social orders designed by any group of people. The founders, however, seem to have been mostly oblivious of the consequences of introducing democracy in a deeply striated society.[5]

Apart from granting universal franchise, the constitution also sought directly to reshape Indian society. The worst features of the caste system such as untouchability were proscribed. The constitution also adopted affirmative action for the "untouchables" by setting aside for them seats in legislatures and jobs in the government—a policy known as "reservations" in the Indian parlance. The cumulative impact of these efforts on the part of the state took some time to register.

Under Jawaharlal Nehru, the Congress won comfortable majorities in the first three general elections of 1952, 1957, and 1962. However, by 1967 the Congress—now led by Nehru's daughter, Indira Gandhi—suffered serious reverses while managing to hold on to a tenuous majority. These elections were the first indication of a social churning initiated by democracy. The poor performance of the Indian National Congress stemmed from the fact that sizable sections of the middle peasantry, which also hailed from the backward castes, had realized the importance of their numerical strength in a democratic system. Hitherto, these groups had voted for the Congress, which remained a party controlled by the upper castes. Now, they preferred to find political formations that supported their interests most closely. The rise of backward caste parties underlines the paradoxical impact of democracy on the caste system. While some of its most reprehensible aspects were ostensibly done away with, caste itself emerged in a political avatar—as a central feature of Indian democracy.

Indira Gandhi attempted to arrest the decline of the Congress by adopting a more radical, populist posture that appealed to the increasingly politically conscious lower orders of society. Indeed, the number of people casting their vote in general elections had almost doubled between 1952 and 1967.[6] Mrs. Gandhi's radical turn fetched handsome rewards in the next general election of 1971, when her party was returned to power on the back of a sweeping majority. The Indian electorate had, however, turned more volatile and assertive. Mrs. Gandhi's political difficulties were coupled with a serious economic crisis touched off by the oil crisis of 1973—an indication of how Indian politics was embedded in a globalizing world.

This conjuncture led to the emergence of a major antigovernment movement. In response, the prime minister invoked the emergency powers of the constitution, setting aside civil liberties and political freedoms for almost two years from mid-1975. The power state was also mobilized against the weakest sections of society, especially through programs of forcible family planning and clearance of urban slums. Although this spell of authoritarian rule was justified in terms of national interests and economic progress, it cost Indira Gandhi dearly when she called for elections in 1977. Despite much of the opposition having been in prison, the Congress party took a major drubbing. The opposition parties that had coalesced into a single anti-Congress front came to power for the first time. The backward castes featured prominently in this coalition. After tasting political power, they also began demanding affirmative action in the form of "reservations" in government employment.

Another important element of this coalition was the party of the Hindu nationalists. This too demonstrated the paradoxical impact of constitutional democracy in India. Although India was ostensibly partitioned on the grounds of religion, the makers of the constitution decided that India would be secular. The establishment of a secular state in a highly religious country, where Hindus constitute some 80 percent of the population, was by any measure a challenging task. Initially, Nehru and his modernizing state seemed to have succeeded. Although communal violence between Hindus and Muslims periodically flared up, the Hindu nationalists' political project of a majoritarian India had little electoral purchase. Starting from 1967, however, the Hindu nationalists began performing well. They played an important role in the antigovernment protests of 1974–1975 and subsequently reaped electoral rewards in 1977.

The coalition that unseated Indira Gandhi proved too unstable, however. In 1980, she returned with a thumping majority. Her assassination in 1984 gave her son and political heir, Rajiv Gandhi, five full years in office. But by the late 1980s, it was clear that the big story of Indian democracy was the rise of the backward castes and the Hindu nationalists. Another interesting development in this decade was the emergence of a prominent party of the former "untouchables" (now referred to as "Dalits" or the downtrodden). These groups had hitherto supported the Congress, but realized that affirmative action needed to be supplemented by political power in order to realize actual change in social relations.

Just as democracy has led to reinscription of caste and religion in public life, it has also resulted in the return of more subtle forms of discrimination against women. Not only were women granted the vote by the constitution, but the Nehruvian state enacted several laws to improve the plight of Hindu women—especially with regard to marriage, divorce, and inheritance. Unsurprisingly, these laws did not result in radical social change. While there was no affirmative action, women were given increasing opportunities for education and employment. Still, a report on the status of women in the mid-1970s found that 68 percent between the ages of 15 and 25 were illiterate, as were 87 percent of older women. Only at the end of the century did female illiteracy drop below 50 percent. Female participation in the workforce remains another problematic area. Between the 1970s and 2000, it was stuck at around 30 percent in rural areas and 15 percent in urban areas.[7] More shocking are the facts that independent India has seen an increase in the ratio of men to women and a rising rate of female feticide.

Democracy in India has led to a considerable widening of participation in public life—unlike many Western democracies there is no voter apathy—but it has not led to the creation of a classic liberal polity where people see themselves primarily as citizens equal before the law. The progress of social reforms under democratic conditions has also been far from smooth or upwardly progressive. On the contrary, the appeal of group identities such as caste and religion has been revitalized in unexpected ways. To be sure, this too has not been an unmixed blessing. The political upsurge of the lower castes has resulted in a "real redistribution of dignity."[8] Even the more recent political triumph of Hindu nationalism has been achieved by yoking this ideology to the politics of backward castes.

ECONOMIC DEVELOPMENT

If the processes of political and social change have been at variance with the predictions of social (especially modernization) theory, economic changes have equally confounded conventional expectations. India entered the twentieth century as a desperately poor country. Between 1900 and 1939, Indian gross domestic product (GDP) grew on average by 1.42 percent every year. Since population over the same period grew by 1 percent every year, growth in per capita GDP during this period was only 0.42 percent. During the interwar period, per capita income was actually stagnant.[9] The dismal economic performance between the wars stemmed from the combination of a sharp upturn in population growth and stagnation of the largest sector (almost half) of the Indian economy, agriculture, which was hit hard by the collapse of global prices during the Great Depression.

At the same time, India was also a significant industrial power outside the Western world. The Great War underscored both the utility of India as a manufacturing base and its limitations. Although the Indian government was granted some leeway to pursue an industrial policy, especially on tariffs, London also sought to protect British goods in the Indian market. As a consequence, Indian industry grew more by expansion than diversification. During the interwar years, while the economy as a whole stagnated, manufacturing output grew annually by almost 4.7 percent.[10] The Second World War provided another fillip to the Indian economy. GDP in real terms expanded during the war years by 10.6 percent. The state played an important role in spurring industrial production. Because wartime shipping restrictions precluded the import of heavy machinery, the Indian economy began to de facto function on the principles of import-substituting industrialization.

The entire apparatus of licenses, permits, and controls developed during the war would be adopted wholesale by independent India.

During the war years, Indian businesses also began pondering their prospects after independence. This led to the publication by leading industrialists of the "Bombay Plan" in 1944. The plan envisaged doubling the per capita income of India from $22 to $45 per annum in 15 years. In the light of wartime experience, it is not surprising that the plan laid maximum emphasis on the development of capital goods industry and infrastructure—sectors in which the state was expected to play the leading part.

The idea of planning was central to the imagination of the postcolonial state. The emphasis in planning was on basic and heavy industries with a view to developing a self-sufficient mixed economy on the lines of import-substituting industrialization. Exports barely figured in plans for the Indian economy. The financial outlay for investment in industry grew from 8 percent in the first plan to 19 percent in the second before touching 24 percent in the third plan (1961–1966). By contrast, the outlay for agriculture hovered around 14 percent in the period covered by the three five-year plans. Nehru hoped that the growing public sector would, in time, generate adequate surplus to be used for mildly redistributive purposes. Between 1951 and 1965, the Indian economy did register significant growth—at an average annual rate of 4.1 percent.[11]

The flaws in the Nehruvian model lay in its mistaken assumptions about agriculture. In the absence of increased investment in this sector, Nehru hoped that the adoption of cooperative forms of agriculture would increase production as well as provide rural employment and cheap food. The cooperative system failed to boost agricultural productivity and generated little by way of rural surpluses for public investment in industries.[12] By the time Nehru died in 1964, the shortcomings of his model of planning were evident. India was increasingly dependent on foreign aid, especially in food. The successive failures of the monsoon in 1965–1966 pushed the country to the brink of starvation.

Internal calamity was compounded by external pressures. The United States—the main source of food grain imports—insisted that

India abandon its experiment in cooperative agriculture and adopt technology-intensive methods that went by the label of the Green Revolution. Indira Gandhi had little choice but to go along. The adoption of the new agriculture strategy paid rich dividends, though it depended considerably on the state subsidizing inputs. Between 1965–1966 and 1971–1972, the production of wheat doubled. The groups that benefited most were the rich and middle peasantry of north India, including the backward castes that were beginning to pull their political weight. The mounting clout of these groups as well as the success of the new methods ensured that agricultural subsidies became a permanent feature of the Indian economy—one that persists to this day.

Following the poor electoral performance of the Congress party in 1967, Mrs. Gandhi embarked on a radical, populist phase: banks were nationalized, businesses closely controlled, and foreign investment tightly regulated. By 1972, industrial activity had begun to perceptibly slow down. The oil shock of 1973 sent the balance of payments sliding down and inflation spiraling up, underscoring the fact that India could not insulate itself from the globalizing world economy. It was against this backdrop that Mrs. Gandhi decided to suspend democracy in 1975.

During this authoritarian interlude, Indira Gandhi's economic policy underwent small but significant changes. Already in mid-1974 she had been forced to seek assistance from the International Monetary Fund (IMF) to tide over balance of payments. Now she began paying more attention to colleagues and prominent industrialists who pressed her to adopt pro-growth policies. Facilitating and accelerating private-sector activity was a key part of the government's economic agenda during the emergency. Big businesses were naturally pleased with this turn in policy.

Economic data bears this out. If we control for the year 1979, when Indian GDP fell by 5 percent owing to the second oil shock following the Iranian Revolution, India's economic growth in the second half of the 1970s averaged a healthy 6 percent. The increase in per capita GDP was accompanied by an increase in productivity owing to higher capital investment. In particular, there was a spectacular rise in private equipment investment since the mid-1970s. Clearly the "animal spirits" of Indian capital were rising from around this time.

This pro-business tilt was continued and intensified during Mrs. Gandhi's last term in office. Economic policy was now focused on raising the profitability of industrial and commercial establishments by easing restrictions on capacity expansion, removing price controls, and reducing corporate taxes. Another important development during this period was the liberalization of electronics imports, particularly of computers. This provided the basis for the subsequent expansion of the telecom and software industries.[13] These policies were continued during the five-year tenure of Rajiv Gandhi. During the years 1981–1988, Indian GDP grew at the rate of 4.8 percent.

Yet neither Indira nor Rajiv Gandhi had the appetite for serious structural reform or unshackling the economy from the state's control. At the same time, they had to cater to the proliferating demands of various politically influential groups—big and small industrialists, rich and middle peasants, government professionals, and the labor aristocracy—that demanded subsidies from the state and brought to bear conflicting pressures on it. The mounting fiscal deficit was initially plugged by dipping into the domestic banking system and later by borrowing on international capital markets.[14] As costs of debt servicing mounted, the government found itself foreign exchange to cover barely two weeks' worth of imports. In turning to the IMF for a bailout, it agreed to initiate far-reaching economic reforms.

By this time, the intellectual case for such reforms to trigger economic growth had become quite strong. The government began freeing up the economy from the regime licenses, permits, and quotas that had survived and intensified from the Second World War onward. More important, it embraced globalization both in terms of foreign investment and exports. Indeed, exports had been a key missing element that accounted for much of the difference between India's economic performance and the East Asian economies during the postwar years.

The reforms of the early 1990s clearly pushed into a sustainably higher growth trajectory. From 1988 to the end of the end of the century, Indian GDP grew at 6.2 percent. In the first decade of the new century, it would begin to touch 9 percent. Interestingly, Indian economic growth during this period was fueled by growth in the services sector, especially the rise of exports of computer software. Further, much of the entrepreneurial energy that underpins the current economic performance of India has come from groups that were historically far removed from India's leading agrarian and commercial communities—many of them stemming from previously marginal castes and social groupings as well.[15]

The standard farm-to-factory-to-office road appears to have been bucked by the pattern of Indian economic development in the twentieth century. This is not unproblematic. Currently, services account for 51 percent of GDP but only 23 percent of the workforce; industry accounts for about 27 percent of GDP and 17 percent of the workforce; and agriculture for 18 percent of the GDP but 60 percent of the workforce. In other words, the most productive sector of the economy employs less than a quarter of the labor force. Moreover, only a tiny fraction are in formal employment or the organized sector. The small size of the industrial workforce—very little of which offers formal employment—is another indicator of the weakness of the organized sector. These peculiarities of Indian development, coupled with the limited fiscal bandwidth of the state, go a long way in explaining the limitations on productivity, the persistence of high levels of poverty—despite the gains of the past couple of decades—and the inability of the state to pursue any substantial welfare policies.

POSTCOLONIAL FOREIGN POLICY

The higher rates of economic growth achieved by the embrace of globalization laid the foundations for India's claims to great power status. This should not, however, suggest that before the last decade of the twentieth century India was an insular state, either in respect of its exposure to global currents or its role on the international stage. At the turn of the twentieth century, India was a crucial strategic asset of the British Empire. The Indian army, financed by Indian revenues, was indispensable to securing imperial interests throughout Asia and large patches of Africa.

Yet, while British India was a cog in the imperial machinery, it was also a significant regional power. The Raj had a sub-imperial system of its own. India's sphere of influence and interference stretched from Hong Kong and Singapore to Malaya and Burma, Tibet and Xinjiang, Afghanistan and southern Iran, Iraq and the Persian Gulf states, Aden and East Africa. Some of these territories had been directly governed by India, while others were dependencies where India's formal and informal writ continued to run. Others still were nominally independent states in which India discerned vital interests or the states' usefulness as geopolitical "buffers."

The various parts of this sub-imperial system were tied to the Raj in different ways: economic, administrative, and cultural. And one form of dependence on India persisted right through: military and security. During the First World War, the Indian army's main effort was focused on the Middle East and East Africa. India's military involvement in the erstwhile Ottoman territories continued in the postwar period. The economic depression and the resultant tightening of financial belts led India constantly to review its military commitments. Yet even before another world war broke out in 1939, the Raj stood ready to defend its own empire. During the Second World War, the Indian army fought in the east in Hong Kong, Malaya, Singapore, and Burma, and in the west in Iran, Iraq, Syria, North and East Africa, the Mediterranean, and Italy.

India's peculiar situation as a colonial entity but also a regional power was recognized in the international system. India was a signatory to the Treaty of Versailles after the Great War. And it was a founding member of the League of Nations—the only non-self-governing entity in the League—and the International Labour Organization. International institutions apart, India was closely tied up with various global currents in the interwar years: pan-Islamism, pan-Asianism, anti-imperialism, communistic international revolutionary anarchism—all left their imprint on Indian politics and were influenced by ideas emanating from India. The jagged rhythms of the global economy during this period also made a deep impact on the trajectory of India. In the aftermath of the Second World War, colonial India was once again present at the creation of a new set of international institutions: the United Nations, the International Monetary Fund (where it acquired one of six permanent directorships), and the World Bank.

As with domestic politics and economics, the foreign policy of the postcolonial state inherited the twin legacies of the colonial state as well as the nationalist movement. This was evident from the outset. As de facto prime minister of the interim government formed in September 1946, Nehru maintained that India was "potentially a great power" and that it was "the centre of security in Asia." This would have delighted the mandarins of the Raj. At the same time, however, he insisted that in foreign affairs India should adopt "an independent attitude with no marked alignment with any group."[16] Here was an adumbration of the idea of "nonalignment" that would come to be closely associated with Nehru's India.

The unspoken assumption in Nehru's thinking was, of course, the unity of India. Following partition in August 1947, India's geopolitical situation was dramatically altered. India could no longer project power and influence in Afghanistan, the Persian Gulf, or the Middle East, let alone Africa. Similarly, the inward turn of Burma rendered moot the possibility of continuing Indian influence in Southeast Asia. In consequence, India's strategic vision narrowed to its immediate horizons. In South Asia, however, independent India continued to adhere to the Raj's vision of being a hegemonic power.

The colonial legacy in foreign policy also impinged on India's ties with its two most important neighbors: Pakistan and China. Soon after independence, India and Pakistan found themselves fighting an undeclared war over the princely state of Jammu and Kashmir—a conflict that would bedevil their relations for the rest of the century and indeed even today. India's relations with the People's Republic of China began more propitiously. Nehru was keen for the two Asian giants to work together and learn from each other's developmental experiences. India acquiesced in the Chinese occupation of Tibet—one of the key "buffer" states for the Raj. But it held on strongly to the boundaries with Tibet and Xinjiang that it believed to have inherited from the British. The Chinese, however, regarded these as a relic of imperialism and sought to negotiate the boundaries afresh.

India's relations with Pakistan and China took shape against the backdrop of the emerging Cold War. No sooner had the Kashmir conflict begun than Pakistan approached the United States for arms, offering in return to act as a shield against the spread of communism in Asia. India, for its part, adopted a stance of nonalignment. This implied eschewing formal military alliances that might pull India into another global conflict; maintaining an independent stance on various international issues and problems; and building autonomous strategic capabilities, a quest that was subsumed under the larger desire to build a self-sufficient industrialized economy. As one of the earliest countries to break free of colonial rule, India also sought to play a leadership role in the newly decolonizing world and foster new forms of solidarity among the Afro-Asian countries and the less-developed world.

Although the United States was irked by India's nonaligned stance, it ignored Pakistan's initial overtures. The onset of the Korean War touched off concerns in Washington about a possible Soviet thrust into the Middle East, and so presented Pakistan in a different light as a useful ally. By 1954, the United States and Pakistan had entered a military alliance—a move that not only intensified the India-Pakistan rivalry but also embittered U.S.-India relations. At this point, the Soviet Union was not a major player in South Asia. Stalin had regarded the postcolonial states as lackeys of the British Empire. Things began to change with his demise in 1953. Thereafter, India and the Soviet Union began edging closer.

This improvement in Indo-Soviet relations occurred at the very time that Sino-Indian relations were nosediving. By early 1959, the boundary dispute was at the forefront of bilateral relations. The simultaneous outbreak of a rebellion in Tibet and the fleeing of the Dalai Lama to India pushed Sino-Indian relations to the edge of conflict. The Chinese believed that India had instigated the rebellion and that it sought to make Tibet an independent state. Moreover, the Chinese believed that the Indians were emboldened in their designs by support from the Soviets. In the years ahead, as diplomacy came to a halt and military clashes occurred on the Sino-Indian frontier, the boundary dispute became entangled in the emerging Sino-Soviet dispute.

The conjuncture of these developments led to a short but sharp war in 1962, in which Chinese forces inflicted a humiliating defeat on the Indian army. At the height of the conflict, Nehru abandoned his earlier concerns and approached the United States for direct military assistance. Nonalignment was weakened to the point of nonexistence. India's claims to leadership in the Non-Aligned Movement received a rude setback. Nevertheless, Nehru believed to the end that India must maintain its ties with Moscow, if only to avoid a close strategic embrace with Washington.

Nehru's successors inherited a fraught security environment in the subcontinent. Not only were India's relations with China and Pakistan deeply problematic, but these two countries also came to form a lasting strategic partnership. In 1965, Pakistan launched a covert operation against India in Kashmir—one that escalated into a three-week all-out war between the two countries. Increasingly embogged in the conflict in Vietnam, the United States, under the administration of President Lyndon Johnson, adopted a "plague on both your houses" stance. This gave the Soviet Union a chance to shape the postwar settlement and ensure restoration of status quo ante. From the mid-1960s Moscow basked in the warmth of its newfound influence in South Asia, attempting to play a balancing role between India and Pakistan and even offering the latter weapons.

The Sino-Soviet clash of early 1969 yet again changed the security situation. Moscow now sought to woo India by offering a long-term treaty of peace and friendship, which would restore the exclusivity of Indo-Soviet relations. Indira Gandhi took it up, but only in the summer of 1971, when India was in the midst of a major crisis originating in East Pakistan. India needed to secure Soviet support not just to deter China from supporting Pakistan, but also to balance against the American "tilt" toward Pakistan emanating from President Richard Nixon's desire for an opening to China. Armed with the treaty, India went ahead to militarily intervene in the crisis and create the independent state of Bangladesh.

In the wake of the 1971 war, India's relations with the United States touched their nadir. The American decision to cut economic aid and, more important, send the U.S. Seventh Fleet into the Bay of Bengal was deeply resented by India. The military move also influenced India's decision to test its nuclear capability in 1974. In turn, the Indian nuclear test imposed additional strains on bilateral relations as the United States imposed a regime of sanctions and denial on India.

By the time Mrs. Gandhi returned to power in 1980, things had begun to change. For one thing, the Soviet invasion of Afghanistan had rejuvenated Pakistan's alliance with the United States. Although Mrs. Gandhi publicly stood by the Soviets, privately she urged them to find an early exit. Simultaneously, she reached out to President Ronald Reagan in a bid to secure a relaxation of sanctions on technology transfers. For another, India's relations with China were on the mend. Deng Xiaoping was eager to detach India from the tight embrace with the Soviet Union, and so suggested a political settlement of the boundary dispute. Although Mrs. Gandhi moves cautiously, India and China began negotiations on the dispute.

Rajiv Gandhi took forward each of these initiatives. Relations with the United States began to look up from the mid-1980s; ties with the Soviet Union were strong but calibrated; and the relationship with China was placed on a new footing by his visit to Beijing in 1989.

Nevertheless, the collapse and implosion of the Soviet Union presented enormous challenges for India. It called into question the continuing relevance of nonalignment and warranted a fundamental reorientation of Indian foreign policy. The fact that this coincided with India's own economic crisis added to the gravity of the situation. In the end, India decided to move both toward globalization and the United States, which, in turn, necessitated diplomatic and economic engagement with U.S. allies in East Asia as well as

Israel. Equally it required jettisoning the old language of solidarity with the less-developed world.

However, the Indian nuclear program—the totem of its continued quest for strategic autonomy—proved a major irritant in ties with the United States. Following India's nuclear tests of 1998, the administration of President Bill Clinton imposed sanctions, though they proved short-lived. The nuclear tests combined with India's impressive economic growth led the United States to view India as a potential strategic partnership. The notion of a "natural" alliance between the world's oldest and largest democracies was invoked to explain this new turn in Indian foreign policy. By the end of the century, India was widely regarded as a major power in the making—one that could help buttress the liberal international order led by the United States.

LESSONS FROM INDIA'S EXPERIENCE

What lessons, if any, can be learned from India's tryst with the twentieth century? With the caveat that history does not teach us any lessons and only historians do, I offer a few suggestions.

First, the idea that liberal democracy is everywhere on the march can be a dangerous illusion. This is an illusion not just in the sense of wishful thinking, but also in the sense of a serious misunderstanding of a phenomenon. The experience of India shows how the particularities of a society and culture shape the working of democracy. This is not to echo the reductive claim that some cultures are unsuitable for democracy. Rather, it is to suggest that democracy could take very different shape in different historical and social contexts. More important, any easy assumptions about helping the spread of democracy must be tempered by the knowledge that the Western experience is unlikely to be replicated in other countries. Indeed, in this respect the trajectory of Indian democracy may teach us more.

Second and related, deep-seated social inequalities or religious identities cannot be erased simply by the forces of modernity—be it the state, market, or new forms of technology. Such embedded institutions and identities tend to find ways of reemerging in modern contexts. Hence, there is no substitute for politics: strategic action by organized groups aimed at securing ever-expanding circles of rights and freedoms.

Third, economic openness and integration are certainly to the benefit of all countries. Yet, in designing global economic institutions or policies, we need to be mindful of the historical peculiarities of countries. India is today seen as a large, emerging economy, but by every per capita indicator it is also a developing country. India may have an advanced software export sector, but the bulk of its population continues to live on the land. Global economic integration can only deepen if we make allowances for such differences rather than demand that one size should fit all.

Finally, India's international experience underlines the point that strategic partnerships might be more useful than rigid alliances in coping with the challenges of the twenty-first century. While offering a measure of enhanced security and the possibility of concerted action, such partnerships do not necessarily abridge the strategic choices of a state or mandate action when critical interests may not be in play. As the world moves toward a global order dominated by the United States and yet consisting of other systemically important powers, not least China, it may be worth revisiting the workings of alliance systems in the twentieth century as well as the history of the nonaligned states such as India.

NOTES

1. From an immense pool of writings, see Shekhar Bandyopadhyay, *From Plassey to Partition: A History of Modern India* (New Delhi: Orient Black Swan, 2004).

2. Erez Manela, *The Wilsonian Moment: Self-Determination and the International Origins of Anti-Colonial Nationalism* (New York: Oxford University Press, 2007).

3. Srinath Raghavan, *India's War: The Second World War and the Making of Modern South Asia* (New York: Basic Books, 2016).

4. Perry Anderson argues that there was nothing unique about the Indian experience: independent Ceylon adopted universal adult franchise a year earlier. He conveniently overlooks the fact that a large group of Ceylonese—Tamils of Indian origin—was actually disenfranchised in the mid-1950s. See Perry Anderson, *The Indian Ideology* (London: Verso, 2013).

5. Sunil Khilnani, *Idea of India* (London: Hamish Hamilton, 1997), 34–35.

6. See Myron Weiner, *The Indian Paradox: Essays in Indian Politics* (New Delhi: Sage, 1989), 196, table 7.1.

7. Dietmar Rothermund, *Contemporary India: Political, Economic, and Social Developments since 1947* (Delhi: Pearson, 2013), 165.

8. Sudipta Kaviraj, *The Imaginary Institution of India* (New Delhi: Permanent Black, 2010), 227.

9. S. Sivasubramonian, *National Income of India in the Twentieth Century* (New Delhi: Oxford University Press, 2000), table 6.10.

10. Ibid., table 6.9.

11. Arvind Panagariya, *India: The Emerging Giant* (New Delhi: Oxford University Press, 2008), 5, table I.I.

12. Francine Frankel, *India's Political Economy: The Gradual Revolution* (New Delhi: Oxford University Press, 2005).

13. Dinesh C. Sharma, *The Long Revolution: The Birth and Growth of India's IT Industry* (New Delhi: HarperCollins, 2009).

14. Anush Kapadia, "The Fiscal Monetary Machine" (unpublished paper, City University, London, United Kingdom, 2014).

15. Harish Damodaran, *India's New Capitalists* (New Delhi: Permanent Black, 2008).

16. *Selected Works of Jawaharlal Nehru*, 2nd ser. (New Delhi: Jawaharlal Nehru Memorial Fund, 1984), 1:438–442n5.

7. GERMANY'S TRAJECTORY IN THE TWENTIETH CENTURY: GLOBAL PERSPECTIVES

Sebastian Conrad

For the most part, historians have framed Germany's modern history in tropes of uniqueness. In this, of course, Germany is itself far from unique. Nevertheless, in narratives of Germany's twentieth-century odyssey, a terminology of the unprecedented and exceptional abounds. Typical tropes include Germany as the cause and originator of two world wars, the singular human crime of the Holocaust, recovery from ashes to riches, the unique invention of a postnational identity, and Germany's role as invisible hegemon in crisis-ridden Europe. There is no doubt that Germany's trajectory through the twentieth century was very specific. However, it is not sufficient to treat Germany as a case sui generis and to try to explain its dynamic essentially from within. The history of Germany was part of the global experience of the twentieth century.

But what twentieth century? And how was Germany linked to larger processes and transformations? In this chapter, I will first sketch three large processes that defined and shaped the twentieth century on a global scale: the history of war and violence, the gradual and then sudden fulfillment of decolonization, and finally the dialectical relationship between globalization and the emergence of macro-regions. In a second step, I will link three crucial moments of the German past—the memory of war and the Holocaust, the role of mobility and migration, and Germany's position within Europe— to these larger processes. In conclusion, I will briefly reflect on how these issues will continue to impact Germany in the years to come, and what new challenges may be on the political agenda in the twenty-first century.

THE TWENTIETH CENTURY IN GLOBAL HISTORY

In many ways, the twentieth century has witnessed cataclysms of unprecedented proportions and transformative events on a scale rarely seen in history. War and violence turned these 100 years into the bloodiest century of world history. The emergence of the global economy linked the livelihood of societies to ever-growing proportions. The political landscape was unified and formatted along the model of the nation-state, at the expense of alternative political entities such as empires, city-states, and territories of mixed sovereignty that had thrived in previous epochs. The pollution of the environment and the destruction of man's natural habitat climaxed at new heights. For the first time in history, hegemonic cultural patterns emerged that people across the world began to reference and engage. Not least, the emergence of the Internet marked a media revolution not seen since the days of the invention of movable types in China and Korea, and the subsequent emergence of the Gutenberg galaxy.[1]

At the same time, many processes were of much older origin. The twentieth century was the heir to developments that reached back deep into the past; at the same time, many of them will continue to exert their influence well into the new millennium. The "twentieth century," in some ways, is thus a very artificial entity that segregates historical time by adhering to the convenience, and convention, of dividing history into slices of 100 years. For many issues, other forms of periodization—some more narrow, others more expansive—may indeed be more appropriate. Scholars have suggested alternatives—narrower periods, such as the Cold War, and broader ones, such as the age of territorialization, the period of colonialism, and the Anthropocene—to capture the different speeds at which history unfolds. Even if we stick to the framework of centuries, opinions diverge. Eric Hobsbawm, famously, has looked at the "short twentieth century," beginning with World War I and ending with the demise of the Cold War regime after 1989.[2] For many issues, however, it will be helpful to go beyond 1989 and to extend our view into the present; this may allow us to assess, and possibly to relativize, the position of the Cold War in current master narratives. It is also more appropriate to begin our study in the 1880s, as this decade was a crucial watershed. It was here that many of the forces that shaped the coming decades—such as the world economy, migrations on a mass scale, high imperialism, the communication revolution, and the rise of Asia—began to take hold.[3] There are thus various ways to define the twentieth century. For what follows, we will keep in mind the fact that it is primarily a heuristic device.[4]

When assessing the dynamics of the twentieth century, both in space (in global perspective) and in time (within the continuity of world history), three large processes in particular can be discerned that, for convenience's sake, we will label as violence, decolonization, and globalization. These are, to be sure, not the only important developments. What is more, they cannot be neatly separated, as all three of them overlap and "spill over" into the terrain of the others. Nevertheless, all three continue to hold sway over the global imagination, making it possible to define individual and collective memories in relation to them. Let us briefly look at all three in turn.

First, there is the history of violence, warfare, and genocide. This is the story that has dominated readings of the twentieth century for a long time. The First World War, frequently dubbed Europe's "original sin," unleashed what is sometimes called "the new Thirty Years' War," culminating in the battles and massacres of the Second World War in which a staggering 65 million people lost their lives. The period of two world wars was followed by what officially was termed the "Cold War," a misnomer and euphemism for a series of conflicts—including such major military events as the Korean War and the Vietnam War—that were localized and relegated to the periphery of the globe-spanning standoff between the United States and the Soviet Union. Some of the bloodiest conflicts were carried out in the form of a civil war, such as the Cultural Revolution in

China that can be understood as intricately related to the Cold War order. Closely linked but not reducible to war were the attempts at genocide—essentially a newcomer on the world stage—that characterized the twentieth century. Genocidal politics—from the deportations and killings of large groups of people in the Balkans and the Ottoman Empire, to the massacre of the Tutsi in Rwanda in 1994—aimed at the physical and biological annihilation of whole people. One of the low points in this century of atrocities was the murder of 6 million European Jews by the Nazi regime in wartime Germany. The Holocaust may appear a German and a European event, but it has gradually been deterritorialized and turned into a site of memory of global proportions; memory of the Holocaust has now been Americanized and also globalized. In January 2005, then secretary-general of the United Nations Kofi Annan celebrated a Holocaust remembrance day at the UN for the first time.[5]

The second large-scale process that recomposed the political landscape globally was the advent of decolonization. The colonial formatting of sovereignty and hierarchy was one of the signature features of global order for many centuries. Beginning with the "discovery" of the Americas, European expansion led to large empires in the Western hemisphere and soon also in Asia and Africa. Imperial formations were not limited to Western powers, as the careers of the Mughal Empire, the Qing, and the Russian Empire attest. In the form of high imperialism, with Germany and Japan as two notable newcomers, the imperial system reached into the twentieth century before gradually dismantling in the postwar period. The quest for independence was not new. It began in the Americas in the early nineteenth century; decolonization became a political agenda in the interwar period (when Germany lost its colonies) and an irresistible movement—for some commentators, a quasi-natural force—after 1945.[6] Decolonization was a political process that instituted an array of formally sovereign nation-states. Beyond the issue of territorial rule, decolonization was linked to initiatives questioning the cultural premises on which the colonial order had been built. Such calls for a decolonization of the mind form one genealogy for current proposals to move beyond a Eurocentric order of knowledge and to reconfigure modernity based on alternative cultural resources.

Third, globalization was one of the master processes of the twentieth century. The term is a new addition to the terminological arsenal employed by historians. Before the early 1990s, it was used very little in public discourse; but from then on, its diffusion became almost epidemic. While the phenomenon was initially seen as radically new, most social scientists and historians now agree that it looks back to a much longer history. We can trace its genealogy back to the beginnings of a capitalist world economy in the sixteenth century; an important phase of acceleration can be located in the final decades of the nineteenth century. From the 1970s onward, and taking off after 1990, globalization transformed the conditions of the world economy and challenged the political logic of world order.[7] At the beginning, the main bone of contention was globalization's effect on the nation-state order. Both the enthusiasts of transnationality and global governance and the skeptics who feared the demise of the nationally organized welfare state held that contemporary globalization is accompanied by an erosion of the nation-state.[8] We now know that a simple dichotomy of globalization and the nation-state is overdrawn. It is more productive instead to focus on another effect that has accompanied the integration of the globe: the emergence of forms of regionalism.

At first sight, the global and the regional appear as contradictory, the assumption being that the latter gradually gives way to the former as communication and exchange increase. Rather than juxtaposing the paradigms of globalism and regionalism, however, it is important to recognize that global integration and the emergence of regional structures have gone hand in hand. Processes of globalization have not led to the emergence of a unified and homogenous world, but have been accompanied by fragmentation and the constitution of difference. The current forms of regionalism—such as in Europe, East Asia, Western Africa, Turkey's Ottoman aspirations, the Americas—therefore need to be seen as an integral component of contemporary globalization and not as an obstacle to interaction.[9] "In the present historical juncture," as Duke University professor

Leo Ching has argued, "regionalisms intercede between the eroding of national autonomy and the deterritorializing of capitalism to reterritorialize transnational capital."[10] The formation of new regionalisms—be it as commercial blocks, as supra-national political entities, or defined in cultural terms as "civilizations"—must be understood as one of the crucial phenomena of the reconfiguration of territoriality under conditions of global entanglements.[11]

These three macro-developments each had their own dynamics and followed their own trajectory. Crucially, however, they also overlapped, and their effects are partly due to the way they interacted and were grafted on each other. The first two processes—the century of atrocities and the Holocaust, and the age of decolonization—are frequently pitted against each other. In this reading, the emphasis on the war and the Holocaust was essentially a Western narrative, not very relevant for the "third world" where the complexities of decolonization, including the many forms of invisible or neocolonialism, mattered much more. However, there are many examples where both readings overlap. The Holocaust has emerged as a normative standard to be tapped into in order to generate global legitimacy, in places ranging from the Ukraine to Kenya and China. Concurrently, both processes are linked when genocide is understood essentially as a product of colonialism and its racializing logic, as can be witnessed in debates about Rwanda and in the continuities between the German genocide of the Herero in present-day Namibia in 1904 and the extermination of the Jews in the 1940s.[12]

Likewise, colonialism and globalization were intricately linked. This refers to the fact that the great empires have in various ways contributed to the process of world integration. The British Empire in particular was a driving force in globalization processes. The majority of global transactions—of goods, capital, labor, and information—occurred within a British-dominated world.[13] Globalization cannot be detached from the colonial structures within which it unfolded; some of these hierarchies survive well into the present.

Intimate links also connected the end of the age of empire and the rise of a globalized world. Both decolonization and globalization

were shaped and strongly influenced by the fundamental transformation of the geopolitical order triggered by the rise of the United
States. The ascendancy of the United States had its roots during
World War I and signaled the beginning of a new global order—
much more than simply the replacement of British hegemony by a
new power. For large parts of the century, U.S. supremacy was challenged by the Soviet Union within the bipolar structures of the
Cold War. After the ideological smoke of the twentieth century has
settled, however, it seems more pertinent to draw a line that con-
nects the gradual demise of the imperial world order, beginning in
the interwar period, to the rise of the United States to dominance
in a globalized world.[14]

The confluence of decolonization and globalization was also the
condition of one of the most remarkable developments of the late
twentieth-century world—namely, the "Rise of Asia." While this
suggestive term ignores the very different trajectories of countries
such as Japan, Korea, and China, it nevertheless alerts us to the
seismic shifts that the global order has witnessed since the 1980s.
It signals the end of Western dominance and thus, broadly speaking,
of the world order created by colonialism. At the same time, it can
be seen as an effect of the regionalizing logic of globalization that
has opened up the possibilities of a polycentric world.

THE GERMAN EXPERIENCE OF THE TWENTIETH CENTURY IN GLOBAL PERSPECTIVE

How did these global processes play out in Germany, and how did
Germany's development impact global structures?[15] For the longest
time, historians have not treated Germany as part of the history
of the world.[16] Instead, they have largely narrated Germany's
twentieth-century journey as an exclusively German story. The
conventional point of departure—the defining moment of Germany's twentieth-century experience—is the Second World War and
the Holocaust. All of the country's prior history is seen in the light
of the war. The long-prevalent plot of the German *Sonderweg*, or de-
viant path, emphasized peculiarity, mustering long-term develop-

ments such as the militarization of society, an authoritarian political system, and anti-Semitism as internal causes that led to two world wars and to the Holocaust.[17]

Germany's postwar trajectory, likewise, appeared as a result of, and response to, the upheavals that the Second World War and the Holocaust unleashed in Germany and beyond. Historians have therefore interpreted the crucial turning points primarily as internal responses to the mid-century calamities. Coming to terms with a past of atrocities and genocide was read as a gradual learning process in Germany's postwar democracy. The 1968 movement was understood as a new beginning, as postwar reloaded, and celebrated as the generational shift that overcame continuities with the Nazi past. Unification in 1990 finally seemed to draw a line under the "German century" of cataclysm and perpetration.[18]

In retrospect, however, it has become apparent that such an internalist story is a myth. Germany was an integral part of global entanglements. In many cases, what appeared to contemporaries as a coming to terms with German guilt was in fact a response to global pressures and to challenges in an increasingly integrated world. For example, the 1968 movement in Germany was intricately linked to similar events elsewhere, Paris and California being the most obvious connections. Contemporary actors referred to Italy and Japan, Turkey and Mexico; they referenced the war in Algeria, Che Guevara, Mao's Cultural Revolution, and the Vietnam War. In Frankfurt and Berlin, "1968" was essentially an instance of the "global 1960s" and not merely a response to the Nazi past. And while the youth movement aimed at toppling hierarchical structures in society and the dominance of capitalist imperialism, it was also part of a global consumer revolution that seemed to contradict some of its rigid ideological claims.[19]

The broad transnational framing of German history is also visible in the other two pivotal developments mentioned previously— Germany's mastery of its wartime past and European integration. One of the key features of postwar Germany has been its gradual coming to terms with the Nazi past and with the role of Germans as perpetrators of war crimes and genocide. After almost two decades of relative silence on the topic, the Auschwitz trials (1963–1965) not only shifted the attention from war and defeat to the issue of the Holocaust, but also signaled the beginning of a more consistent and self-critical stance vis-à-vis the nation's past. Through reparations paid to Holocaust survivors and the gradual extension of compensation to other victim groups, (West) Germany assumed moral and legal responsibility for its past atrocities. This redemptive policy found symbolic expression in public acts, such as the genuflection of German chancellor Willy Brandt in Warsaw in 1970, and the apologies of President Richard von Weizsäcker in his much-acclaimed speech in 1985. Most commentators as well as scholarly works portray "Vergangenheitsbewältigung" (coming to terms with the past) as an achievement of (West) German postwar democracy and as the result of a collective learning process. Internationally, Germany serves as a model for postconflict reconciliation. Domestically, Germans have embraced the politics of atonement that now appears as one ingredient of Germany's peculiar form of postnational nationalism.[20]

Rarely discussed, however, is the extent to which Germany's mastery of the past was not the result of German developments alone. In fact, it was significantly shaped by a multifaceted transnational constellation. Debates about the past bore the traces of a globalizing world, deeply engraved in what is often still perceived as the realm of the uniquely national, of a peculiar mentality and mind-set. These transnational factors included direct interventions, such as by the United States during the occupation immediately after the war, or by the Jewish Claims Conference, founded in the 1950s to negotiate compensation for Holocaust victims and their offspring with German authorities. More important than direct pressures, however, was the integration of the Federal Republic into the Western camp in the Cold War setting (and the concomitant distancing from Eastern Europe). This process implicitly rested on a reading of the past that was compatible with the expectations of the international community.

This pattern is most clearly visible in the context of the emergence of Europe as a political and institutional reality. Political and economic integration required an alignment of different and competing views of the past. This was not in any way a formalized process—even if today denial of the Holocaust is considered a formal obstacle to accession to the European Union (EU). More important are the implicit (and sometimes explicit) pressures exerted by media and public spheres to work toward a harmonization of different understandings of the past. In this respect, the German example is no exception. The Eastern expansion of the European Union saw intense debates in Poland about Polish complicity in the Holocaust. The discussion about Turkish membership, in turn, has put the 1915 massacre of the Armenians squarely on the table—not only in Turkey itself, but across Europe, most notably in France. For better or worse, admitting to one's crimes and a politics of official apology have emerged as internationally recognized testing grounds for the maturity and reliability of a nation. While this mechanism is particularly prominent in Europe, it is as clearly visible in Australia, in the United States and her relationship to slavery and the repression of American Indians, and in East Asia.[21]

What has been hailed as a coming to terms with the past, and thus as a relation in time (between past atrocities and later commemoration), must then instead be understood as a response to transnational and global challenges. What is now celebrated as an achievement was also an effect of the particular European and Cold War context in which Germany found itself. But whatever way we look at it—coming to terms with the past as a unique German accomplishment or as the product of a confluence of forces—as a political strategy it has served Germany well. It has helped to reintegrate the country into the international community. By programmatically adhering to a foreign policy based on contrition and apology, Germany has been able to link an ethical commitment to humanist causes and mutual understanding, with a realpolitik of integration into the Western alliance. All this has facilitated, if not enabled, Germany's move from international pariah to respected partner and economic wunderkind, and to the status of one of the three leading exporting countries in the world that has emerged as the political and economic engine of the European Union.

The process of European integration, and Germany's role within it, was of course itself predicated on larger geopolitical contexts. This is the third moment to be considered here. After having been excluded from European institutions in the aftermath of the war, West Germany pursued a path of "Westintegration," or rapprochement with the Western alliance, thus postponing the political goal of national unification to the faraway future.[22] In the 1950s and 1960s, Germany—paradoxically—could only gain sovereignty by partly giving up claims to sovereignty and by integrating into the institutional structures in Western Europe and the Atlantic world. Similarly, unification in 1989–1990 was only possible through carefully calibrating national aspirations, European realities, and global contexts. For Chancellor Helmut Kohl, anchoring a united Germany firmly within the organizations of the Western alliance was a foundational premise. But, at the same time, there was not much of a choice. The formation of a united and substantially enlarged Germany in the midst of Europe was only palatable to the Western powers by inserting it more firmly than ever before into the net of European institutions. One of the prices to pay was relinquishing the currency and assenting to the adoption of the euro as collective currency. Put more generally, the creation of the European Union as well as the geographical enlargement and the increasing penetration of its organizational structure were the conditions under which the powers accepted unification. Much more than the fulfillment of a national teleology, unification was to a large extent a European and global event.[23]

More than that, embedding Germany within Europe was not only the result of a conscious strategy. To be sure, a series of influential German politicians has consistently championed the European cause and worked toward closer institutional bonds within the community. Likewise, governments in many European countries (and also in the United States) have seen it in their best interest to further political and economic integration and thus hold Germany in a friendly embrace. Indeed, these are the stories conventionally told: the European Union was the result of an emerging European consciousness and resolution never to tolerate war on European territory again, and the result of a strategy of containment of a potential German threat.

What these two narratives downplay, however, is the extent to which the emergence of the European Union in the 1990s was also a response to global challenges. As we have seen, the end of the Cold War and the demise of the bipolar world order, together with the onset of globalization, triggered the formation of larger regional entities around the world. In many ways, the European Union was one, albeit prominent, manifestation of this larger trend. As a result of geopolitical reshuffling and the unprecedented linking of markets globally, structural pressures emerged toward regional alignment that cannot simply be reduced to a long-term political master plan and to idealist visions of European harmony.

Seen in this light, the founding of the European Union in 1993 through the Maastricht Treaty was also not just the fulfillment of a long-standing promise, the pinnacle of a development that began in the interwar period and then found institutional form in the 1948 Hague Congress and the establishment of the European Coal and Steel Community four years later. While the conventional narrative emphasizes continuity over time and the gradual growth of a germ that in its earliest stages already contained the full European potential, this is only half of the story. To be sure, the creation of monetary unity and further steps toward a European federation in the 1990s would not have been possible without a prior history of institution building. There was of course an element of path-dependency, but at the same time, the European Union was also the product of the very specific global conditions in the wake of the Cold War. This was, then, not primarily a continuation, but just as important, a new beginning, conditioned by global geopolitical transformations and new structures of global capitalism.

INTO THE TWENTY-FIRST CENTURY

When asked about the significance of the French Revolution, the Chinese premier Zhou Enlai famously quipped that it was "too soon to say." Similarly, assessing the twentieth century shortly after its calendrical completion is in many ways premature. History, in particular the history of the recent past, is a moving target: interpretations of the past 10 decades have shifted considerably after the watershed moments of 1989 and 1991, after September 2011, and then again following the financial crisis in 2008. Interpretations are bound to change in the future as well. Moreover, drawing on the experience of the twentieth century cannot simply serve as a guide to the twenty-first. The future is never merely the projection of past trends into the future. That said, it is likewise true that there is no absolute beginning, and that powerful transformations are at work that prestructure future events and will be with us for some time.[24]

Viewed from a German/European vantage point, the three themes and problematics that we have discussed are likely to continue to shape developments in the decades to come. The way in which they have an impact on societies, however, may shift as these issues are negotiated in an increasingly global world. This is certainly true for the first theme: war/violence and memory. As the Second World War recedes into the deep past, and as survivors with a firsthand experience of the war and its atrocities are passing away, one might assume that demands for apologies and compensation will gradually disappear from the public agenda. Paradoxically, however, the reverse is true. Indeed, claims on the past continue to proliferate, as more and more social groups campaign to have their suffering and victimization recognized. Currently, we witness many similar movements emerging in societies around the world. In many cases, claims are formulated primarily domestically, as marginalized and downtrodden groups pressure for an awareness of past wrongdoings and for an inclusion of their memory into national narratives. Frequently, ethnic groups such as the first nations in the Americas and Australia voice these concerns. This is not, however, exclusively a national/ethnic agenda; demands for reconciliation are a much broader phenomenon, as the creation of forums for the negotiation of diverging experiences and memories in many postconflict societies, ranging from Eastern Europe to South Africa and Latin America, vividly attests.[25] In other cases, demands for atonement and financial settlements are staged in the international arena, such as in the case of slavery and the memory of colonial suppression and violence.

Increasingly, however, the two spaces overlap, as memory activists instrumentalize the international arena for national agendas, and vice versa. They form broad transnational coalitions that add to the dynamics and to the political weight of campaigns, not least by implicating different public spheres and by appealing to a potentially global audience. As the global has emerged as the defining arena for political actors, ranging from nation-states and transnational institutions to grassroots movements, these actors see themselves compelled to engage with a globalizing public sphere. In Germany, debates about the country's role in the Armenian genocide and about the 1904 massacre of the Herero in what is present-day Namibia are among the examples of this new and worldwide phenomenon.

The process of globalization has instilled the calls for apologies and compensation with an added urgency. Migrants carry their memories with them and insert them into novel social and political contexts. In addition, the communication revolution has multiplied the publics to which memory activists can appeal, thus adding to the force, and the potential resonance, of their claims. More fundamentally, globalization has shifted the terrain on which controversies over public memory are played out. With the disappearance of the East-West dichotomy, the clear-cut framework that endowed all events with political meaning has vanished. In many respects, the symbolic conflicts over the meaning of the past have moved into its place and been substituted for the ideological antagonisms. As a result, we can speak of a virtual "explosion" of memory in many places around the world in the decades after 1990. After the alleged "end of history" (at least the end of a history dominated by universalist projects), the unceasing discourse on the past corresponds with a post-ideological economy of signs. In a world unified by capitalist globalization, with no political alternatives on the horizon, history and memory now constitute a symbolic site where struggles over geopolitics and global justice are fought out.[26]

Similarly, the ongoing processes of decolonization and regionalization interact in complex ways with the pressures of a globalizing world. Colonialism remains one of the privileged angles from
which to understand the complexities of global integration. Politicians and scholars alike detect the roots of globalization in the long
history of colonization.[27] And while globalization promises an end
to the hierarchical structures of the West and the Rest, powerful
claims have also been made to the effect of attributing current inequalities to the path dependency initiated by the extractive politics of Western colonial rule.[28] Whatever the final verdict on this
issue will be, it is clear that some of the conflicts caused by current
transborder movement and circulation have their deep roots in the
colonial past. The massive migration of people from formerly colonized countries is a crucial example. It seems clear that migration
from poor countries will continue to pose a dramatic challenge to
many parts of the industrialized world in the years to come. Both
an economic and a social issue, large-scale mobility will change the
makeup of both "sending" and "receiving" countries, to use euphe-
misms from the social science literature. In the United States and
in the European Union, the social pressures caused by the conflict
surrounding inward mobility have not only led to the fortification
of borders, but also to contested debates about the future fate of the
community. In important ways, mobility (not least by refugees)—and
the controversies surrounding it—is beginning to change what
"Europe" or "Germany" means.

If applied more broadly, the notion of decolonization refers not
only to territories formerly ruled by imperialist powers, but more
generally to a world order defined by the hierarchies established by
Western hegemony and its universalist projects. In this sense, the
rise of countries like Brazil, India, and China, all emerging from
dependent positions within the political economy of the past two
centuries, likewise contributes to shifts in the geopolitical status
quo. While thus challenging the colonial legacies engrained in
today's world order, the emergence of new economic and political
powers also feeds into the process of regionalization so character-
istic of our days.

A case in point is the much-diagnosed return of religion as one of the signature features of the globalized present. The "return of the Gods" undoubtedly marks one of the seismic shifts in public culture in many parts of the world, ranging from the waves of Pentecostalism in Latin America and Africa to the return of "indigenous" religions, the revival of Islam and Hinduism (and their incarnation as right-wing political ideologies), and the quest for alternative religions linked to nontranscendental practices. While thus signaling new forms of spirituality and subject formation, the rise of religions has also emerged as a powerful political force. Muslim brotherhoods and Islamist movements, Christian fundamentalisms, the Indian Bharatiya Janata Party (BJP) and its Hindutva ideology, and terrorist groups such as al Qaeda all attest to the new political role that religious ideologies and milieus play. Many commentators thus underline the changing political culture in many places and the shifts in legitimate political discourse. It is more productive, however, to understand the rise of religion as one of the incarnations of the emergence of regionalisms in the post–Cold War world.[29]

Part of the popular appeal of the return of religion lies in the challenge it poses to the hegemony of Enlightenment rationality and the secular notion of modernity. Indeed, the emphasis on alternative cosmologies and indigenous epistemologies is staged as an assault on the cultural dominance of the West. In this opposition, it is heir to earlier attempts to break away from Western universalism and posit radical alternatives grounded in autochthonous traditions. Such genealogies notwithstanding, the current challenges to the Western script are very much the product of the dynamics of globalization and the calls for a multipolar and multicentered world.

In crucial ways, then, forces that have their origin in the past centuries continue to shape the present and future. Many developments—among them the memory of war/violence, the decolonization of the Western-dominated world, and the emergence of regionalism—look back to a long history that remains crucial to any attempt to understand their dynamics. In some ways, then, the twentieth century supplies the script for the twenty-first.

But the reverse is also true. Future developments will decide what the relevance and significance of the past will have been. While recognizing the power and thrust that comes with this long gene-alogy, it is just as important to recognize the way in which the cur-rent conjuncture is the product of synchronous forces on a global scale and cannot be deduced from historical trajectories internal to individual societies alone. It may thus well be that, retrospectively, we will read the twentieth century as part of the Anthropocene—the age beginning with the Industrial Revolution in which humans began to dramatically change the climatic conditions on the planet and turned into a geological agent.[30] Surely, balancing the relation-ship between man and nature and devising ways of sustainable growth without imposing insurmountable debts on future genera-tions will be among the crucial challenges of the years to come. Whether we will come to see the rise of an ecological consciousness, and not war, the Holocaust, and the end of colonial rule as the chief legacies of the twentieth century, it may indeed be too soon to say.

NOTES

1. For overviews of the history of the twentieth century, see Mark Mazower, *Dark Continent: Europe's Twentieth Century* (New York: Vintage Books, 2000); Wil-liam R. Keylor, *The Twentieth-Century World and Beyond: An International History since 1900*, 6th ed. (New York: Oxford University Press, 2011); and Michael H. Hunt, *The World Transformed: 1945 to the Present*, 2nd ed. (New York: Oxford University Press, 2016).

2. Eric Hobsbawm, *The Age of Extremes: A History of the World, 1914–1991* (New York: Pantheon Books, 1994).

3. For such a perspective, see also Charles S. Maier, "Consigning the Twentieth Century to History: Alternative Narratives for the Modern Era," *American Historical Review* 105 (2000): 807–831; Michael Geyer und Charles Bright, "World History in a Global Age," *American Historical Review* 100 (1995): 1034–1060.

4. For a discussion of the meaning of a century (using the nineteenth century as an example), see Jürgen Osterhammel, *The Transformation of the World: A Global History of the Nineteenth Century* (Princeton, NJ: Princeton University Press, 2014), 45–77.

5. Hilene Flanzbaum, ed., *The Americanization of the Holocaust* (Baltimore: Johns Hopkins University Press, 1999); Peter Novick, *The Holocaust in American Life* (Boston: Houghton Mifflin, 1999).

6. John Darwin, *Britain and Decolonization: The Retreat from Empire in the Post-War World* (New York: St. Martin's, 1988); Prasenjit Duara, ed., *Decolonization: Perspectives from Now and Then* (New York: Routledge, 2004); James D. Le Sueur, *The Decoloniza-*

tion Reader (New York: Routledge, 2003); Martin Shipway, *Decolonization and Its Impact: A Comparative Approach to the End of Colonial Empires* (Malden, MA: Blackwell, 2008). For the quasi-natural force of the process, see Stuart Ward, "The European Provenance of Decolonization," *Past & Present* 230 (2016): 227–260.

7. Jürgen Osterhammel and Niels P. Petersson, *Globalization: A Short History* (Princeton, NJ: Princeton University Press, 2009); Anthony G. Hopkins, *Globalization in World History* (London: Pimlico, 2002); Andrew Hurrell, *On Global Order: Power, Values, and the Constitution of International Society* (Oxford: Oxford University Press, 2007).

8. David Held, Anthony McGrew, David Goldblatt, and Jonathan Perraton, *Global Transformations: Politics, Economics, and Culture* (Cambridge: Polity Press, 1999).

9. Peter J. Katzenstein, *A World of Regions: Asia and Europe in the American Imperium* (Ithaca, NY: Cornell University Press, 2005); Oleksander Pavliuk and Ivana Klympush-Tsintsadze, eds., *The Black Sea Region: Cooperation and Security Building* (Armonk, NY: M. E. Sharpe, 2004).

10. Leo Ching, "Globalizing the Regional, Regionalizing the Global: Mass Culture and Asianism in the Age of Late Capital," *Public Culture* 12 (2000): 233–257, quotation on 243.

11. Andrew Gamble and Anthony Payne, *Regionalism and World Order* (New York: St. Martin's Press, 1996); Louise Fawcett and Andrew Hurrell, eds., *Regionalism in World Politics: Regional Organization and International Order* (Oxford: Oxford University Press, 1995); Arif Dirlik, *Global Modernity: Modernity in the Age of Global Capitalism* (Boulder, CO: Paradigm, 2007).

12. Donald Bloxham and A. Dirk Moses, eds., *The Oxford Handbook of Genocide Studies* (Oxford: Oxford University Press, 2013).

13. James Belich, *Replenishing the Earth: The Settler Revolution and the Rise of the Anglo-World, 1783–1939* (Oxford: Oxford University Press, 2009); Gary B. Magee und Andrew S. Thompson, *Empire and Globalisation: Networks of People, Goods, and Capital in the British World, c. 1850–1914* (New York: Cambridge University Press, 2010); John Darwin, *The Empire Project: The Rise and Fall of the British World-System, 1830–1970* (Cambridge: Cambridge University Press, 2009).

14. David W. Ellwood, *The Shock of America: Europe and the Challenge of the Century* (New York: Oxford University Press, 2012); Adam Tooze, *The Deluge: The Great War, America and the Remaking of the Global Order, 1916–1931* (London: Allen Lane, 2014).

15. For overviews of German history in the twentieth century, see Hans-Ulrich Wehler, *Deutsche Gesellschaftsgeschichte*, vols. 4 and 5 (Munich: C. H. Beck, 2003–2008); Eckart Conze, *Die Suche nach Sicherheit: Eine Geschichte der Bundesrepublik Deutschland von 1949 bis in die Gegenwart* (Munich: Siedler, 2009); Ulrich Herbert, *Geschichte Deutschlands im 20. Jahrhundert* (Munich: C. H. Beck, 2014).

16. For the postwar period, the primary focus here will be on the Federal Republic.

17. On the Sonderweg narrative, see Stefan Berger, *The Search for Normality: National Identity and Historical Consciousness in Germany since 1800* (New York: Berghahn, 1997). For a critical perspective, see David Blackbourn and Geoff Eley, *The Peculiarities of German History: Bourgeois Society and Politics in Nineteenth-Century Germany* (Oxford: Oxford University Press, 1984).

18. For the argument of the "learning process," see Daniel J. Goldhagen, *Hitler's Willing Executioners: Ordinary Germans and the Holocaust* (New York: Knopf, 1996).

19. Carole Fink, Philipp Gassert, and Detlef Junker, eds., *1968: The World Transformed* (New York: Cambridge University Press, 1998); Norbert Frei, *1968: Jugendrevolte und globaler Protest* (Munich: Deutscher Taschenbuch Verlag, 2008); Samantha Christiansen and Zachary Scarlett, eds., *The Third World in the Global 1960s* (New York: Berghahn, 2013); Martin Klimke, Jacco Pekelder, and Joachim Scharloth, eds., *Between Prague Spring and French May: Opposition and Revolt in Europe, 1960–1980* (New York: Berghahn, 2011); Martin Klimke, *The Other Alliance. Student Protest in West Germany and the United States in the Global Sixties* (Princeton, NJ: Princeton University Press, 2011); Arthur Marwick, *The Sixties: Cultural Transformation in Britain, France, Italy, and the United States, c. 1958–c. 1974* (Oxford: Oxford University Press, 1998); Stephan Malinowski and Alexander Sedlmaier, " '1968'—A Catalyst of Consumer Society," *Cultural and Social History* 8 (2011): 255–274; Qinn Slobodian, *Foreign Front: Third World Politics in Sixties West Germany* (Durham, NC: Duke University Press, 2012).

20. On Germany coming to terms with the past, see the overview by Peter Reichel, *Vergangenheitsbewältigung in Deutschland: die Auseinandersetzung mit der NS-Diktatur von 1945 bis heute*, 2nd ed. (Munich: C. H. Beck, 2007). See also Sebastian Conrad, *The Quest for the Lost Nation: Writing History in Germany and Japan in the American Century*, trans. Alan Nothnagle (Berkeley: University of California Press, 2010).

21. Aleida Assmann and Sebastian Conrad, eds., *Memory in a Global Age: Discourses, Practices, and Trajectories* (New York: Palgrave Macmillan, 2010); Daniel Levy and Natan Sznaider, *The Holocaust and Memory in the Global Age* (Philadelphia: Temple University Press, 2006).

22. Heinrich August Winkler, *Germany, the Long Road West, vol. 2, 1933–1990* (Oxford: Oxford University Press, 2007).

23. Kiran Klaus Patel, "Germany and European Integration since 1945," in *The Oxford Handbook of Modern German History*, ed. Helmut Walser Smith (Oxford: Oxford University Press, 2011), 775–794; Peter Katzenstein, *Tamed Power: Germany in Europe* (Ithaca, NY: Cornell University Press, 1997); Mereike König and Matthias Schulz, eds., *Die Bundesrepublik Deutschland und die europäische Einigung, 1949–2000: Politische Akteure, gesellschaftliche kräfte und international Erfahrungen* (Stuttgart: Steiner, 2004).

24. On the role of long-term perspectives in history, see Jo Guldi and David Armitage, *The History Manifesto* (Cambridge: Cambridge University Press, 2014).

25. Alexandrea Barahone de Brito, Carmen Gonzáles-Enríquez, and Paloma Aguilar, eds., *The Politics of Memory: Transitional Justice in Democratizing Societies* (Oxford: Oxford University Press, 2003); David Hirsh, *Law against Genocide: Cosmopolitan Trials* (London: Cavendish, 2003); Pheng Cheah, *Inhuman Conditions: On Cosmopolitanism and Human Rights* (Cambridge, MA: Harvard University Press, 2006). For a legal perspective, see M. Cherif Bassiouni, *Crimes against Humanity: Historical Evolution and Contemporary Application* (Cambridge: Cambridge University Press, 2011).

26. Roy L. Brooks, ed., *When Sorry Isn't Enough: The Controversy over Apologies and Reparations for Human Injustice* (New York: New York University Press, 1999); Elazar Barkan, *The Guilt of Nations: Restitution and Negotiating Historical Injustices* (New York: Norton, 2000); Michel-Rolph Trouillot, "Abortive Rituals: Historical Apologies in the Global Era," *Interventions* 2 (2000): 171–186; Yumiko Iida, "Between the Technique of Living an Endless Routine and the Madness of Absolute Degree Zero: Japanese Identity and the Crisis of Modernity in the 1990s," *positions* 8 (2000): 423–664; Janna

Thompson, *Taking Responsibility for the Past: Reparation and Historical Justice* (Cambridge: Polity, 2002); John C. Torpey, ed., *Politics and the Past: On Repairing Historical Injustices* (Lanham, MD: Rowman & Littlefield, 2003); John C. Torpey, *Making Whole What Has Been Smashed: On Reparation Politics* (Cambridge, MA: Harvard University Press, 2006); Mark R. Amstutz, *The Healing of Nations: The Promise and Limits of Political Forgiveness* (Lanham, MD: Rowman & Littlefield, 2005); Manfred Berg and Bernd Schaefer, eds., *Historical Justice in International Perspective: How Societies Are Trying to Right the Wrongs of the Past* (New York: Cambridge University Press, 2008); Danielle Celermajer, *Sins of the Nation and the Rituals of Apology* (New York: Cambridge University Press, 2009); Fatima Kastner, *Transitional Justice in der Weltgesellschaft* (Hamburg: Hamburger Edition, 2015).

27. Magee and Thompson, *Empire and Globalisation*.

28. Daron Acemoglu and James A. Robinson, *Why Nations Fail: The Origins of Power, Prosperity, and Poverty* (New York: Crown Business, 2012).

29. Mark Juergensmeyer, *Global Rebellion: Religious Challenges to the Secular State, from Christian Militias to al Qaeda* (Berkeley: University of California Press, 2008).

30. Dipesh Chakrabarty, "The Climate of History: Four Theses," *Critical Inquiry* 35 (2009): 197–222; Julia Adeney Thomas, "History and Biology in the Anthropocene: Problems of Scale, Problems of Value," *American Historical Review* 119 (2014): 1587–1607.

INDEX

Abe, Shinzo, 35–36, 45
Acheson, Dean, 25
African Americans: racism and, 15,
  29–31, 120; in World War II, 22
agenda. *See* global agenda, government
  with shared
AKP Party (Justice and Development
  Party), 55
Algeria, 50, 64–65
alliances, power and, 32
Anderson, Perry, 106n4
Annan, Kofi, 111
Arabs, xi, 51, 54, 64–65
Armenia, 51, 56, 62, 117, 121
Asquith, Herbert, 37
al-Assad, Bashar, 59, 66
Atatürk, Mustafa Kemal, 51, 59
Atlantic Charter, 21, 24, 73
atonement, 116, 121
Auschwitz trial (1963–1965), 116
Australia, 29, 89
autarky, 41, 44

Beasley, W. G., 38
Bharatiya Janata Party (BJP), 5, 123
Bolshevism, 7, 10, 72
"Bombay Plan," 96
Boot, Max, 16
Borgwardt, Elizabeth, 21
Bosnia, with genocide of Muslims, 53,
  64, 65
Boxer Rebellion, 70
Brandt, Willy, 116
Bretton Woods, x, xiii, 8, 9, 23
Brown v. Board of Education, 29
Burma, 100, 101

Canada, 89
caste system, in India, 91–92, 94–95
Cecil, Robert, 40
Center for Strategic and International
  Studies (CSIS), vii, 1
Ceylon, 106n4
Chamberlain, Joseph, 37
Charleston church massacre, 31
Chen Duxiu, 71
children, viii, 25; female feticide, 94;
  Wagner-Rogers Bill and Jewish, 18
China, 9, 17, 50; Chinese Communist
  Party, 8, 71, 72, 73; in context, 69–70;
  economy, ix, 4, 70, 80–83; global
  conflicts and, 5–6, 7, 71, 73–74; as
  global power, 2, 38, 83; Great Prole-
  tarian Cultural Revolution, 78,
  110–111; Korean War and, 75; May
  Fourth Movement, 40; military, 103;
  with nationalism, rise of, 70–74;
  People's Republic of China and
  "new," 74–80; politics and, 26, 79–81,
  84, 85n13; protests in, 10, 81–82; Qing
  dynasty, 4, 38, 70–71; Sino-Japanese
  War of 1894–1895, 38, 70; Sino-
  Japanese War of 1937–1945, 43, 73;
  with Tibet and colonization, 101–102;
  today, 82–84
Chinese Communist Party (CCP), 8, 71,
  72, 73
Chinese Revolution of 1911, 71
Ching, Leo, 113
Churchill, Winston, 21, 73
"City on a Hill" (Winthrop), 14, 15, 29,
  33n1
climate change, xii, xiii

ABOUT THE EDITORS AND CONTRIBUTORS

Cemil Aydin is an associate professor of history at the University of North Carolina at Chapel Hill.

Sebastian Conrad is a professor of history at the Freie Universität Berlin.

Michael J. Green is senior vice president for Asia at the Center for Strategic and International Studies and chair in modern and contemporary Japanese politics and foreign policy at Georgetown University in Washington, DC.

John J. Hamre is president and CEO at the Center for Strategic and International Studies in Washington, DC.

Yuichi Hosoya is a professor at Keio University in Tokyo, Japan.

William Inboden is an associate professor at the Lyndon B. Johnson School of Public Affairs at the University of Texas at Austin.

Chen Jian is Hu Shih Professor of History and China-U.S. Relations at Cornell University in Ithaca, New York.

Shinichi Kitaoka is professor emeritus at the University of Tokyo in Tokyo, Japan.

Srinath Raghavan is a senior fellow at the Center for Policy Research in New Delhi, India.

Nicholas Szechenyi is a senior fellow and deputy director of the Japan Chair at the Center for Strategic and International Studies in Washington, DC.

ABOUT CSIS

For over 50 years, the Center for Strategic and International Studies (CSIS) has worked to develop solutions to the world's greatest policy challenges. Today, CSIS scholars are providing strategic insights and bipartisan policy solutions to help decisionmakers chart a course toward a better world.

CSIS is a nonprofit organization headquartered in Washington, D.C. The Center's 220 full-time staff and large network of affiliated scholars conduct research and analysis and develop policy initiatives that look into the future and anticipate change.

Founded at the height of the Cold War by David M. Abshire and Admiral Arleigh Burke, CSIS was dedicated to finding ways to sustain American prominence and prosperity as a force for good in the world. Since 1962, CSIS has become one of the world's preeminent international institutions focused on defense and security; regional stability; and transnational challenges ranging from energy and climate to global health and economic integration.

Thomas J. Pritzker was named chairman of the CSIS Board of Trustees in November 2015. Former U.S. deputy secretary of defense John J. Hamre has served as the Center's president and chief executive officer since 2000.

CSIS does not take specific policy positions; accordingly, all views expressed herein should be understood to be solely those of the authors.